Sexuality and Human Values

SEXUALITY AND HUMAN VALUES

The Personal Dimension of Sexual Experience

EDITED BY

MARY S. CALDERONE
Executive Director, SIECUS

A Siecus Book

ASSOCIATION PRESS / New York

International Standard Book Number: 0–8096–1891–5
Library of Congress Catalog Card Number: 74–22119

Library of Congress Cataloging in Publication Data

SIECUS Conference on Religion and Sexuality, St Louis, 1971.
  Sexuality and human values.

  Bibliography: p. 157.
  1. Sexual ethics—Addresses, essays, lectures.
  2. Sex instruction—Addresses, essays, lectures.
  I. Calderone, Mary Steichen, ed. II. Sex Information
  and Education Council of the U. S. III. Title.
  HQ31.S12   1971   301.41'7   74–22119
  ISBN 0–8096–1891–5

Contents

Moral Reasoning and Value Formation

Evaluation and Prospect

Introduction

The purpose of the SIECUS Conference on Religion and Sexuality,* out of which this book comes, was to bring together primary researchers in the fields of sexuality and of values. To meet with these researchers, the three major faith groups and various denominations were invited to choose members from their own communities who would be interested in joining in dialogue about the materials that the researchers had presented. It was felt that such an opportunity for free give-and-take might provide religionists with the data that would give them a common basis for fresh viewpoints on the many dilemmas confronting society in the field of sexuality and human values.

The researchers, who had specific topics assigned to them, had much the easier task. The taped discussions following each presentation revealed by the questions from the floor that the participants had a real wish to hear accurately and to understand what the researchers were saying. These question-and-answer periods have been drawn upon, but have not been included *in toto*.

On the last day of the Conference, after the researchers had taken their leave, came the opportunity for the religious participants to enter into dialogue with one another about the presentations. It was then that it became apparent that the Conference had not been structured in such a way as to facilitate definitive actions or conclusions. Rather, the research presentations had served to highlight a number of doubts and anxieties that happily appeared not to focus on sinful man (as might have been expected even twenty years ago) so much as on today's residual reluctance of formalized religion to deal more positively with sexuality. It seemed as if the clergy were caught in the same trap as are so many troubled human beings of living in an open, pluralistic society bombarded from without by contradictory messages regarding sexuality and values, and from within by their own convictions and urgings.

During the various dialogues several issues were highlighted. In spite of the lack of resolution, some of them have been put

---

* Held October 17–19, 1971 at St. Louis, Mo.

down here. The editor and the publisher then elected to invite
John L. Thomas to write a concluding chapter that would, by as-
saying the nature of the "fertile zero" that Father Thomas identifies as the stopping point of the Conference, lay the groundwork
for what is still needed from religion as regards human sexuality
and sexual behavior.

In the opinion of the editor, what is still needed remains
much as it was before the Conference took place: the absolute
and increasingly urgent necessity for the churches once and for
all to comprehend the true sexual nature of humankind. This is
far different from the imagined or presupposed, or stereotyped or
insisted upon, sexual patterns that religion has, with all good intentions, been foisting on human beings for so many centuries;
an image that is not only untrue and contrary to the facts but
that damages human beings when they try to force themselves
into its rigid mold. Because this mold is so far from fitting real
people, these efforts always end in failure, which in turn causes
further pain, guilt and ensuing damage.

What is this false image? Primarily, that the sexual nature
of the human being ought not to exist, and is therefore to be
suppressed until maturity and marriage have been achieved, when
it is suddenly to emerge in full flowering. But this is simply not
the way human beings work. And the researchers, at this Conference, did their best to present to the religious community the
basic truths about how sexuality really develops.

Briefly, sexuality begins in the uterus when, due to the elab-
oration of male hormone around the end of the second month
of gestation, the sexual brain centers of those embryos that are
genetically male receive their masculinizing messages, as do more
visibly their genital structures. In the absence of androgen effect,
all embryos will differentiate as female. At birth the sexual ap-
paratus, whether male or female, is (like other organ systems of
the body) ready to function—and does so within the first twenty-
four hours, as Masters points out.

Following sex assignment at birth, the culture then takes
over and with messages and programming from parents and other
adults in the child's environment continues masculinization or
feminization of the baby.

The erotic drive, which seems to cause everyone so much

trouble, is present in greater or lesser degree at birth, to the extent that the arousal-plateau-orgasmic sequence described by Masters and Johnson for adults has been reliably observed in quite young infants. Now, and during childhood, is where a powerful negative cultural influence interposes itself via the parents and others. Religion has influenced society over and over again to indicate, succinctly and forcefully, that sexual pleasure is under no circumstances to be derived from the body by the child who inhabits that body. In other words, the parents are led to interpose themselves between the child and his or her own body with the constant message, often reinforced by punishment or threats of punishment, that the child does not own its body, which would appear to belong to the parents. These early messages create a societal set of mind that has been disastrous to the sexual lives of countless individuals since earliest Christian times. Even so, the erotic drive persists throughout the life cycle.

Simplistically perhaps, the scientist asks: "Since no harm has been demonstrated to come from the expression of sexual self-pleasure, except the guilt inflicted on the individual for this, why go on with the futile exercise of attempted repression, especially in view of the damage these efforts have been shown to cause? Why should succeeding generations of children, adolescents, and young or older adults, be deprived of enjoying that with which they were endowed?" This question extends to many forms of sexual behavior at other times in life, including the later years. It is no longer sufficient for the churches to state that "sex is good" and is "God's gift to us," both of which statements I firmly believe, if they then proceed to hem sex in with attitudes and restrictions that prevent its full flowering.

This is not to deny the high desirability, as was pointed out several times, for all of us to develop a system of moral values and, above all, of consciences, and to apply these to sexual, as to other behavior. But the mythologies about sex simply have to go, whether we be church people or science people—or both. There are too many other shibboleths in modern society that need clearing away, to permit continued existence of the ridiculous ones that hem in or distort this one human faculty—especially one so important in the evolution of people toward full capacity to relate to each other in warmth, tenderness, care and joy. In particular, it is the fear of the erotic in human behavior that has to go.

Right here is where I find it easiest to shift my focus from the understanding of eroticism as a scientist to the celebration of it as a religious person. Perhaps this is because of my Quaker persuasion. In any case, I find that I simply cannot convince myself that the erotic aspect of human life is not as truly integral to "that of God in every person" as is, for instance, the intellectual, the cognitive. Descartes' *I think, therefore I am* can not today be considered complete without the complementary *I feel, therefore I am*. And, except for the electively celibate, *I feel, therefore I am* almost inescapably requires consideration of the erotic.

Other religions have incorporated such celebration into their ethical systems. Many are notable for the peacefulness of their cultures and their human relationships, as ours is not. Thus, whether as scientists or as religionists, we should be seeking to make it possible for human beings to realize their erotic potential in full and responsible conscience. The energy now required to maintain the wasteful blockage by fear and guilt of the erotic could then be freed for creative purposes in the life of humankind. Surely the achievement of Kohlberg's sixth stage of moral reasoning by an increasing proportion of the population would help serve to release these blocked energies.

Some denominations and, indeed, some individuals in all the faith and denominational communities have already begun such celebration on behalf of, and with, the people they serve, if only by their positive attitude about sexuality. Such positive action can best serve to counteract and bring into balance the many sexually negative, exploitive elements on the one hand, and the many fear-inducing, life-denying elements on the other. Perhaps this conference served to break some ground here, and if, after reading this book, some consensus on further action can be reached within the religions, the "fertile zero" state of the Conference at its close might actually mark a true beginning on the needed tasks described by Father Thomas in the final chapter.

The Conference on which this book is based was in part supported by grants from Mr. J. Noel Macy, from the Patrick and Aimee Butler Family Foundation, and from the W. Clement and Jessie V. Stone Foundation, whose executive director, Mr. H. Rhea Gray, contributed much helpful counseling.   M.S.C.

Gender Identification

Heterosexuality

CARLFRED B. BRODERICK *

Any discussion about gender identity and heterosexual and homosexual development might usefully begin with the three aspects
of sexual development first recognized by Brown and Lynn
(1968).

One is *gender identity*: Am I male? Am I female? The work
at the Johns Hopkins Gender Identity Clinic and elsewhere suggests that gender identity is achieved by the child very early. Their
data show that by the age of 2½ or 3 years, it can be damaging
as well as difficult to try to change a child's sexual identity. Suppose, for example, a physician should find a newborn baby to be
of ambiguous sexual structure, with a sex organ too big for a
clitoris and not quite big enough to be a penis; but the parents
finally decide to name him Jim, because they have always wanted
a boy. Then, when the child is older, the doctor decides that Jim
will never develop as a functional male, but, with surgery and
hormones, can be made into a functional female.

The question: What is the latest age at which this kind of
fundamental switch in gender identity can be made without trauma
to the child? The answer: It gets tougher and tougher after about
age two. It staggers the imagination to realize how well we teach
children their gender. My three-year-old son, for example, has
for quite a while been very sure that he's a boy and that he'll
grow up to be a daddy.

* Carlfred B. Broderick, Ph.D., Department of Sociology, University
of Southern California, Los Angeles, Calif.

Separate from gender identity but often confused with it is *gender role behavior,* or socially defined masculinity and femininity. Since this is socially defined, it changes over time. For example, thirty years ago when the Minnesota Multiphasic Personality Inventory (MMPI) was developed, it included a scale intended to measure masculinity and femininity. But, in the last thirty years, the social definitions of masculinity have so shifted that today the average male scores many points higher in the direction of femininity than did the average male of thirty years ago. In fact only one third of those males of thirty years ago would have scored as high in the direction of femininity as does today's *average* male, and only one sixth as high as today's *college* male.

But are college males less masculine than they were? No, the change has occurred in our cultural definition of masculinity. For example, there is an item asking whether you would rather go to a concert than stay home and work on your car. That's not necessarily effeminate any more: the culture permits masculine males this kind of preference. Similarly, a female who would rather speak up and make an independent contribution at a meeting than sit back and be a listener used to score as "masculine." In today's world we let women be more aggressive and independent.

So masculinity and femininity are socially determined, and vary from culture to culture. They also vary within our own culture, for we live at a time when dramatic shifts in what constitutes femininity are occurring. (I was having breakfast with a lady to invite her to write an article for the *Journal of Marriage and the Family* on sexism in family studies. At the end of the breakfast, a very awkward moment came. I'd invited her to eat with me to discuss this proposition and I didn't want to do the gauche thing under these circumstances, so I said, "Well, would you mind—that is, how would it square with your view of our roles if I picked up the breakfast tab?" She said, "You know, I've been thinking about that ever since you invited me." I said, "Well, how are we coming? What did you finally decide?" She said, "The key questions is this: Would you pick up the tab if I were a man?" I said, "Good heavens, yes. I invited you; it's a business conference." "All right," she said.)

Masculinity and femininity are being redefined on every side. On the other hand there would seem to be no justification to go the whole way and say there are no longer any important sex-role differences. That is just not true. We observe manifest and significant differences between boys' and girls' behavior, even though these are different differences from formerly. It may well be that they are fewer, but certain important and significant differences continue. The boy who has a high voice and a walk that reminds us of the way women walk, and who is perhaps not athletically inclined, has a hard row to hoe. And a girl who comes across flatfooted and direct and square in her gestures and in her presentation doesn't get the same response as does a girl who is built and behaves more as we think girls ought to be built and behave.

Masculinity and femininity, in turn, need to be distinguished from heterosexuality and homosexuality. A generation ago, if a young man had mannerisms that were considered effeminate, the common thing to do was to label him a "fairy." If he also wore orange socks on Thursday, that was an infallible sign! But today's research has shown us that, aside from the "queens," (that group of male homosexuals who force their homosexuality to the notice of others), the large majority of homosexuals are in the same range of body build, personality style, and so on, as the large range of heterosexuals. The stereotype that you can tell a homosexual by the way he walks and talks, and the way he gestures, is manifestly untrue except for the aforementioned small group of "queens."

The fact is that homosexuality is not related to masculinity. A football player, masculine by social definition, may still be homosexual; and a male can be effeminate or "precious" in the way he behaves and minces, and yet be heterosexual through and through.

The Homo-Hetero-Sexual Choice

Having made those distinctions, we can now talk about heterosexuality and how it develops. It is important at the outset to point out that we have no certain knowledge as to what leads some people into heterosexuality and others into homosexuality.

But certainly our culture works very hard to force everybody to be heterosexual and succeeds to a remarkable degree, if you take marriage as a criterion. For the fact is that 95 per cent of us get married. For that matter, since almost 10 per cent of our population are preferential homosexuals, according to the data of Kinsey and others, it must be assumed that at least half of the practicing homosexuals are married. So we really do a big sell on getting people married. Some fifteen years of my own research have been devoted to tracing the sequence of events by which people decide, finally, that they want to get married. What we do must be terribly efficient, especially since in our culture we don't rely on other people's efforts to get us married. One way or another we manage to have one of the highest marriage rates in the world. How do we do it?

The process is already well under way by the time the child is in kindergarten. What do children at this age think about marriage? Are they heterosexual? Are they homosexual? Or are they latent? Or not interested in sex at all? Few parents will be surprised to know that in nursery school and kindergarten, over half of the girls are sure they're going to get married some day. Most nursery-school children probably have very little notion of the sexual part of heterosexuality, but they know grown-ups live in male and female pairs. However, if girls in nursery school are sure they're going to get married, boys aren't so sure. They have the same examples put before them, but it's clear that boys are steered differently, are less carefully oriented toward *marriage* than girls. Instead, boys are carefully oriented toward *sex,* not by their parents, who presumably wouldn't take that responsibility, but by their male contemporaries, who work hard and do a very good job of it, from the older boys right on down the line.

By the time girls are twelve, over 90 per cent of them are sure they want to get married, and eventually they do just that. Boys are a little slower to come along, and this depends on the culture, too. For example, black males at every age are less enthused about marriage than are white males of the same age, and they get progressively less enthused the older they get. They are the only group that actually gets less interested in marriage between the ages of fourteen and seventeen, when others are getting more interested in marriage, suggesting perhaps that there is some counter-marriage socialization going on in the black male peer group. By the time white boys get out of high school, about 75 per cent of them want to get married some day, as contrasted with only 50 per cent of the black boys.

Back at twelve years of age, it will be remembered, over 90 per cent of the girls had already decided. What happens? The girls win, of course. But 95 per cent of the boys get married, too! How do we manage that?

The Role of Fantasy

Well, as soon as a child decides he is going to get married someday, it appears that this triggers a whole sequence of events in his life, beginning with fantasies. Think back to the days of your own fantasies. In my case, I remember, my crushes had very few social consequences. My fantasies ran to the James Bondish—you know, zapping through the world, women falling dead from admiration on all sides. At that age I lacked altogether his sense of what to do with these swooned women when they had fallen. There was no question of the heterosexuality of these fantasies, however, and I suspect that many of you recall similar early fantasies.

One of the strongest counts against Freud's concept of childhood latency is that there is no period at which social fantasies involving the opposite sex are not romantic in content. That is, rarely, at any age, do boys think about girls, without thinking about them differently from the way they think about boys. That is not something acquired later in life. It is built into the assumptions of our culture, and children are very quick to pick this up. When they are very young, their fantasies are uncomplicated and simplistic. For example, things always go right in these fantasies—the couple always get along perfectly and live happily ever after. When children get a little older, social circumstances develop so that they must test out these fantasies against real social experience with girls. From that point on, the stories and the fantasies begin to change. They become more realistic, the characters get more worried. It might be assumed that the opposite would be the case. With more experience, it might seem that they would feel more competent and that their fantasies would reveal a comfortableness with the other sex. The opposite is the case, however. Before they had any experience, they were sure that everything would go well; but when they actually got together with real girls they didn't know what to say and they worried that the girls might not like them. In actual practice the ones they liked didn't like them back, and they made big fools out of themselves trying to make jokes that didn't go over. So then they started to worry about what to do with girls.

Interestingly, however, the older the boys get, the more likely they are to risk finding out. In fourth grade, for example, only about 10 per cent will have the experience of being chosen as the sweetheart of the girl whom they have selected to be the object of their affections. To that limited extent their fantasy has a degree of reality. The rest is all in their heads. By the time they get to high school, almost no boy will say, "She is my girl friend," without the assurance that she will also say, "Yes, I am his girl friend." By then having a sweetheart is more social process with real social consequences. The fantasy is subordinate to the social reality.

The Shift to Reality

How do children make this shift into the real social world? Data gathered from sixteen elementary school districts spread through Georgia, Pennsylvania and Missouri lead to the conclusion that kids' fantasies constitute a kind of rehearsal. You have, perhaps, observed this in your own children. I have a teenager who postures in front of the mirror. She turns this way and that, and says sophisticated things to herself as though in conversation with a boy. She doesn't like the way it sounded that time, so she tries it with a different inflection, and with her head tilted just a little.

I say, "Honey, what makes you think the boy is going to give you the straight line so you can say this rehearsed thing?" She looks coldly at me, like "Don't worry," and I don't doubt but what she finds a way of working in that line she's been rehearsing all week.

Young children do the same thing. They rehearse the kinds of roles that they think they're going to have when they're older. Love, for example. That's a very important emotion. How does the child find out what the content of being in love is? The answer is, he falls in love, of course. Among fifth graders, 50 per cent of them are now in love. Also 50 per cent of the sixth graders and seventh graders, also eighth, ninth, tenth, eleventh and twelfth graders. How do you explain the fact that roughly 50 per cent of every age group, with little variation, are always in love? Well, I'll give you one other datum. If you ask them when they first fell in love, at each age level, it turns out to have happened just within the last year. How would you explain such a datum? This gave us a terrible time, trying to understand what had happened the year before we did our study, so that half the world fell in love.

It is our guess that it's because everybody defines this year's love as being real love, and last year's doesn't count. If you ask a seventh grader, "What about when you were in love in the fifth grade?" he answers, "What did I know about love in the fifth grade? Now that I'm more mature, *now* I know about love." I had a roommate who did that all the way through college. Every six weeks, he fell in love for the first time and he always put down the last one as just practice. "I didn't know what love was until I met Mary Ann," he said one day, as he put Joan's picture in the drawer.

Now, that's rehearsal. That's practice. Kids do it at least from the fifth grade on in large numbers. And we all do it. My students always ask me for a definition of love. They're very serious-minded about this. They want to check themselves against my list of criteria. I always tell them that I can give them the foolproof definition of love, which they can write down and with which they can pass any exam. Love is that emotion you feel in your current relationship. I think that's an unchallengeable definition. Former "loves" were mere practice and rehearsal.

We practise and rehearse social skills as well as emotions. My own very first experience at a kissing game was at a Sunday-school party. I was a very self-righteous young man and much above worldly things like kissing parties. For two or three years I had managed to dodge them and I submit that I had every right to expect to keep my virtue intact at a Sunday-school party. I think things started that night with the young people hazing the comparatively young couple who were our chaperones, trying to get under their skins, saying, "Let's play kissing games." This was a super-righteous young couple also, just my kind of people. Well, naturally they were so offended that everybody increased the pressure for the project until, finally, the couple left because they wouldn't be parties to this. A couple of the other super-righteous kids left. I almost left, but I wanted to see if they really would do this at a Sunday-school party. You see, I was a researcher even then.

And so there I was ready to take notes. But you can anticipate, I am sure, that it didn't work out at all as I had thought it would. It's a wonder I didn't give up scholarly pursuits altogether. In the first place, they went out in the kitchen to do this kissing. If you were a skeptic, as I was, would you believe they were really out there kissing at a Sunday-school party? I had serious doubts. And, secondly, I had not fully anticipated that I would turn out to be a participant-observer. On about the third spin the bottle turned toward me, and then toward old Sally Heims who was the same shape as the bottle. (It was a milk bottle too, not a Coke.) I remember going out in the kitchen with her and it was a very awkward moment when we faced each other, inside the doorway. I said, "Do you think those other kids were really kissing when they came out here?" She turned very coy, which I thought ill became her, and said, "Well, I guess you'll just have to figure that out for yourself." I didn't like her attitude, so I went home.

But what is a kissing game, after all? It's an opportunity to practice kissing just for its own sake. You don't choose the girl. She doesn't choose you. You have to be a good sport, unless you're a super-righteous, insecure type as I was. You don't get much of a chance to louse it up because you have to come back from the kitchen after a while so somebody else can go out and use the kitchen. There is very little ego risk. Kissing games are just to get practice in kissing so that when it really counts on a private enterprise basis, you know how to do it.

We rehearse, then, because we don't want to mess up when we get into a real situation. We rehearse emotions, we rehearse commitments. I was talking to the leader of a rock group one time on an airplane while on my way out to California, and he gave me an insight that I had certainly lacked before. I had never understood those women who faint and shriek and go all orgasmic over pop performers. Men don't do that. They'll pound and whistle and so on, but it's not the same as this female ecstasy. When I was a kid, it was Frank Sinatra and the bobby-soxers, and before that it was the Sheik. After Sinatra, it was Elvis Presley and then the Beatles. Anyway, these boys traded on that, and this leader explained it to me in a way which seemed to contain a very real insight in terms of fantasy as rehearsal. He said they used to do one-night stands (between gold records) on high-school stages, which usually weren't air-conditioned and they would sweat a lot. Now, you can short out an expensive steel guitar if you get to sweating heavily, and so they would carry towels to mop their foreheads with. Accidentally, they discovered that these sweat rags had erotic significance for the girls in the audience. Girls would come up after the performance and ask, "Will you give me your sweat rag? I'll take it home and I'll put it under my pillow and I'll never wash it." And so they would say, "Sure, be my guest."

Well, they decided to build it into their act. So as the last number of the evening they would sing some provocative song—you know, the "Come on and get it, honey, I'm going to give it to you good" type. And they'd hang these rags out over the footlights. On a good night the girls would get up in the aisles and shriek and scream and yell and reach for these rags. In the final, final moment, the rock group would throw these towels out to the girls who then screamed louder and would tear the things to shreds and each take a piece home and put it under her pillow, I presume.

They got so good at this that they had to count on cordons of self-sacrificing police to keep the girls back—that was the only way they could preserve themselves. But one night, in Akron, Ohio, the girls got through the police barrier. At the crucial moment the police apparently thought of their wives and families and decided not to sacrifice themselves in this way, and let the girls come pouring onto the stage. The guys in the band were scared to death. They had visions of being torn apart, earlobe from toenail and pressed under girls' pillows.

Can you guess what actually happened? Nothing! Nothing at all happened! Those girls got up on the stage and suddenly saw five quivering boys in front of them—real, live boys—and they turned right around and went down off the stage. That wasn't part of the deal. Until that moment of confrontation, it was all fantasy; it was all a script written in their own minds where it was perfectly safe. *He says this and I do that,* and even if it's a terrible risqué and exciting and dangerous thing, a girl has complete control over it. It's just as dangerous as she wants it to be. She can change her mind and revise the script later if she wants to. But she can't do that with a real boy. He not only might take advantage of her, but he might reject her, he might think her dull and uninteresting, he might think the next girl is cuter and leave her standing there. Real boys don't follow the script in a girl's head at all, but if she can keep them on the stage or in a picture tube or on a film, then she can count on them.

And so, girls apparently have more need for safety than boys, and they rehearse passion in their heads with more enthusiasm, because of the safety, I suppose.

To summarize, young people rehearse. They rehearse emotions, commitments, social behavior, at different ages depending on their social maturity.

The Move Into Heterosexuality

Contrary to some people's expectations the most popular kids are the ones who start first. It is not a case of those boys and girls who are least secure with their own sex group taking up with the opposite sex as a compensation. Just the opposite is true. The boys who are most in with the cliques, who are most socially active and on the most teams, and chosen first at baseball, are the fellows who also make the first moves heterosexually. Apparently they get support from their same-sex peers. They aren't defectors from a jealous monosexual clique. Rather, it seems that peers approve of making a move toward the girls, and then, of course, coming back to the peer group. The boys who have the fewest heterosexual fantasies, who don't even think about girls very much, tend to be the shy ones who are not active in groups. They're not the kids who are making it in the monosexual world.

It is true, of course, that young people move out heterosexually at different ages. Some start at the age of ten, eleven or twelve; some do not start until they are in their teens. Eventually they move through the stage of fantasies and rehearsal into a socially designed vortex of intimacies and commitments in pursuit of their concept of the adult role.

It is true also that in addition to the romantic component which we have discussed here, there is the development of explicitly sexual interests—especially among boys.

Alfred Kinsey found that almost no males have ever discovered masturbation for themselves, but lots of females have. We must assume that this difference is not due to any deficiency in the boy's ability to be sexually imaginative. Rather, the opportunity of discovering it for one's self is a casualty of the fact that nearly all of one's friends are happy to explain it seriously or more likely through jokes and tricks. "Hey, kid, sit down in this chair." "Okay." "Now, pretend that you picked up a cat in the street." "Okay, yeah." "Put it in your lap." "Yeah." "You've got a knife there. Now stab it six times. Ha, ha, ha, look at him jacking off." There is scarcely a chance for a boy to discover masturbation for himself, with all this help. There's always a "dirty Arthur" in the fourth grade who instructs males in the ways of the world. Girls get less help of this type.

The point is reinforced by a study done in the Psychology Department at Penn State. The department showed male and female students, one by one, three different sets of words that flashed tachistoscopically, very fast, while their palmar sweat (an index of excitement) was measured electrically. It was found, as you might expect, that the first set, containing words like "home" and "love" and "child," didn't excite anybody. These were good safe words.

Then there was shown a set of really bad words—four-letter words—and, as you might expect, both girls and boys recognized them as exciting words and the needle jumped for everyone.

Then a set of words that were capable of ambiguous construction—words like "lay," "come," "screw," "make," which had both a sexual and a nonsexual meaning—was shown. When a girl saw "lay" flash up there, she apparently thought "chicken" and the needle didn't move. But when a fellow saw "lay" he thought "chick," a different species. The needle jumped for him as it didn't jump for the girl. Now, that's due to training, not hormones. That's perceptual differentiation: a boy is more trained than the girl to see the sexual potential in ambiguous situations.

This differential training of females primarily for marriage and secondarily for sex, and of males primarily for sex and secondarily for marriage produces an exchange vortex that leads to full sexual intercourse, and to marriage, in an order determined by such factors as values, relative advantage, and bargaining strategies that deserve an entirely separate analysis and discussion. But the important thing is that it seems to work; 95 per cent of us do get married and that is the ultimate expression of our heterosexual socialization.

Homosexuality

JUDD MARMOR *

What we still don't know about the subject of homosexuality is almost unimaginable. It is an area in which all kinds of strong prejudices, feelings of abhorrence, contempt and anxiety exist, so that opportunities to study the homosexual community as comprehensively and objectively as we must do in order ultimately to understand its members fully, have been lacking.

Yet it is important for us to recognize that these antagonistic feelings, so widespread in our own society, are not universal in today's world, nor have they existed in all cultures and at all times. In the majority of human societies homosexuality actually has an acceptable place and is regarded with abhorrence or abjured in only about one third of them.

A Definition of Homosexuality

A major problem that complicates the discussion of homosexuality is that of definition. For example, homosexuality can be defined in a purely functional or behavioral sense as *sexual relations between any two members of the same sex.* But the moment you begin to analyze that behavior, this explanation becomes inadequate because people have relations with members of the same sex for a wide variety of reasons. Individuals who are primarily

* Judd Marmor, M.D., Director, Divisions of Psychiatry, Cedars-Sinai Medical Center, Los Angeles, Calif.

heterosexual in their inclinations may engage in homosexual behavior because they are deprived of heterosexual opportunities for unusually long periods of time; other individuals who define themselves as primarily heterosexual may nevertheless engage in homosexual behavior for money; others do so because they are lonely and want affection from whatever source they can get it; still others do so out of boredom and the desire to try something new, or from a feeling of rebelliousness and contempt for the conventional mores of our society. And then, of course, there is the homosexual behavior of adolescents, which is usually an exploratory kind of thing, and is not a true preference; most adolescents would prefer heterosexual explorations, but because of our cultural mores those avenues are often less accessible to them.

It is thus more meaningful to define homosexuality as "a strong and sustained preferential erotic attraction to members of the same sex." It should be seen as analogous to the sustained preferential erotic attraction to members of the opposite sex that characterizes the state of heterosexuality. Once homosexuality is defined in such terms, it becomes clear that it is perfectly possible for an individual to have powerful homosexual *inclinations* and yet never indulge in homosexual *behavior,* whether out of guilt or anxiety, the same reasons for which many lonely heterosexuals never find or make the opportunity for heterosexual contact.

A still further complication to any definition of homosexuality is the fact that heterosexuality and homosexuality are by no means clear-cut entities. Kinsey constructed a scale of 0 to 6, in which zero represents exclusive heterosexuality and six represents exclusive homosexuality, with the intermediate stages falling in between. When the actual sexual behavior of human beings is studied on this scale, it is found to cover a wide spectrum of behavior between the two extremes.

The fact that homosexuality probably occurs in all societies is important to keep in mind. From the writings and graphic arts of the most ancient civilizations it is clear that homosexual behavior existed in those times also. It is, however, extremely difficult to get accurate statistics about its incidence, particularly in those cultures in which it is disapproved. We do know that it occurs in all walks of life, at all socioeconomic levels, among all racial and ethnic groups, in rural as well as in urban areas, and among professionals as well as among working men and women. There is no area of our contemporary life that does not have some individuals who engage more or less exclusively in homosexual behavior.

Kinsey's figures showed that 37 per cent of all American males have had at least one homosexual contact at some time or other in their lives. This figure probably ought to be corrected for two factors: one is homosexual behavior in prisons, most of which is the forced homosexual behavior of heterosexuals that really does not constitute the kind of homosexuality we are talking about. The other factor is adolescent homosexual contacts. Controlling for these two factors, and eliminating those whose contacts have been relatively rare, would give us a more accurate figure, which seems to be borne out by studies throughout the world. This is that at least 4 per cent of all males, and at least 2 per cent of all females, are more or less exclusively homosexual throughout their adult lives, *i.e.,* they would fall somewhere between 4 and 6 on the Kinsey scale.

When you think about it that's a pretty large number of people! In terms of our present American population, this means perhaps as many as 10 million American males and perhaps 5 million American females. Moreover, Kinsey's figures indicate that at least 10 per cent of American males have been more or less exclusively homosexual for at least three years of their lives. Another figure that has been lost in the mass of Kinsey's statistics, but that is very interesting for reasons that I shall expound a little later, is that an additional 13 per cent of males react erotically to other males even though they have never had any homosexual experiences at all after adolescence. This is very significant because it shows that the potentiality for homosexual experience or for homosexual arousal is really quite widespread.

The Homosexual Choice

Now, what is it that makes individuals become more or less exclusively homosexual in the face of the powerful hetero-sexual acculturational influences our society provides? There are many theories of the etiology, which is a good indication that we still don't have a definitive answer. Freud believed that all human beings were basically bisexual. He based this on the fact that the early embryo has bisexual structures and therefore he thought that human beings were all psychologically bisexual as well. He believed that everyone went through a phase of homosexual development, and if he or she became arrested at that phase through some kind of faulty development, or regressed to that phase because of subsequent anxieties, homosexuality would ensue.

This theory of bisexuality is not widely held today among sophisticated biological scientists because of our improved knowledge of genetics. Even though it is true that there are male and female structural components in the young embryo, we now know that from the moment of conception, in the vast majority of human beings, there is a clear-cut genetic differentiation as to whether we are XY, which makes us male, or whether we are XX, which makes us female.* There is no valid reason to assume, therefore, that there are biologically determined psychological components of the opposite sex inherent in all of us.

As a matter of fact, many of the assumptions about such biologically determined femininity and masculinity refer to aspects of gender identity which we now know are not genetically fixed, but are subject to strong cultural modification. For example, Freud assumed that males were biologically destined to be aggressive and females to be passive, and that masculine interest in athletics, and feminine interest in esthetics were also biologically determined. Today, we know that these patterns are largely, if not totally, the results of acculturation processes.

Biological theories about homosexuality are still in a state of confusion, although until a few years ago it was thought that the problem was pretty well settled. We do know that no significant genetic differences can be demonstrated between homosexuals and heterosexuals. We also know that *by ordinary tests,* no sig-

---

* Recent biological research indicates that there is a critical period in the prenatal development of lower mammalian males in which the hypothalamic centers are "sensitized" by the action of foetal androgenic hormones. This early sensitization seems to be of major importance in determining subsequent adult sexual behavior patterns. Whether this is also true in humans still remains to be determined, but there is some suggestive evidence that it may be. This could be relevant in some homosexual and transsexual patterns.

nificant hormonal or chromosomal differences can be shown. However, in recent years, some researches have been done that at least have opened wide again this question of a possible biological component to homosexuality.

We have to go back to rats for some of the evidence. While it is important to issue a careful *caveat* in that you can't transfer the findings from rats to human beings too easily, there is a certain prototypal reaction that may be significant. Dorner (1967), a German endocrinologist, some years ago demonstrated a fascinating thing: He castrated male rats at birth and when they became adults he injected them with testosterone, the male sex hormone. When this was done, these rats, who until that time had been uninterested in sexuality, became very interested in it *but in a female manner; i.e.,* they presented themselves "effeminately" to normal male rats in a receptive copulatory posture. On the other hand, when he castrated male rats at birth but on the third day following gave them a *single* small injection of testosterone, then, when he gave them replacement male hormones when they had reached adulthood, the rats behaved in a normal copulatory manner with females, mounting them in the usual masculine way.

This is a fascinating finding, because it suggests that at some point in the development of the young organism, at least in lower animals, a sensitization process takes place, probably in the hypothalamus (part of the midbrain) which creates a predisposition toward male or female sexual behavior. I should warn you again that we cannot directly apply this to human beings, but it has raised the question of whether some such sensitization may take place in human beings, either in the intrauterine period of life or at some key period after birth. Among other studies suggesting a possible endocrinological basis for homosexuality the most provocative are those by Kolodny, Masters et al. (1972), who demonstrated that Group 5 or 6 homosexuals seem to have a deficiency in plasma testosterone. It must be emphasized, however, that these studies have not yet been replicated and cannot be considered as proven.

All we can say at this point is that they have again opened up the question as to whether or not, in some cases, there may be some biological predisposition to homosexuality. It is important, however, not to assume that these studies indicate that people are born homosexual. This is not true. All that can be adduced from this, if substantiated, is that some individuals may be born with a *predisposition* that, given subsequent reinforcement from environmental influences, may make them more susceptible than others to developing in a homosexual direction. This does not negate what is still the most commonly accepted view about the development of most homosexuality (which is an adaptational view); namely, that sexual object choice is a postnatal, biographically *learned* matter, and that individuals who learn an aberrant or variant sexual choice, have done so for reasons in their life experience that have either blocked the path to normal heterosexual acculturation for them or, for some reason or other, have facilitated the path toward the aberrant sexual choice.

Factors Blocking the Heterosexual Choice

It is important to recognize one very significant fact. Exclusive heterosexuality, contrary to what many people believe and what we are often taught, is not a "natural" thing. Studies of higher primates and, indeed, of lower mammals too indicate that although it's perfectly true that heterosexuality is the preferred adaptation in a state of nature (obviously it would have to be for species to survive), nevertheless it is never exclusive. Both higher primates and lower mammals often engage in behavior which is unmistakably homosexual, so much so that biologists talk of natural behavior in primates as being ambisexual; in effect, bisexual but with the more frequent goal being a heterosexual one. Exclusive heterosexuality and exclusive homosexuality are unique human by-products that are the results of specific acculturation processes. The vast majority of us are programmed to be exclusively heterosexual, but a small proportion become exclusively or almost exclusively homosexual through variant forms of acculturation.

How is the sexual choice toward heterosexuality blocked? It can be blocked in a number of different ways, by virtue of which the capacity of the child to make a satisfactory identification with the parent of the same sex and a loving and trustful adaptation to, or relationship with, the parent of the opposite sex is interfered with. This is true for both males and females.

One of the most common of such patterns is an overly seductive or controlling mother and an absent, distant or unloving father for the boy. In such a situation, the boy's path toward heterosexual development may be blocked by guilt in relationship to the seductive mother, which brings up all kinds of incestuous anxieties; or by fear of being overwhelmed by a controlling and overly protective mother; and also by his failure to develop a satisfactory sense of his own maleness, of his own capacity to be a male, because of the failure to have adequate modeling behavior in relationship to a loved father. But that isn't the only type of family constellation encountered. A father who is an overwhelming father, who seems too much to possibly identify with, may make a young boy feel totally inadequate and incapable of modeling himself after him, and he may choose then to be closer to the mother and model himself after her, in various ways that are both conscious and unconscious.

There is some evidence that homosexuality may sometimes be positively learned, and is not alone the results of fears or inhibitions toward the opposite sex. We occasionally see individuals who very early in their lives, in childhood, were introduced to sexual gratification by a member of the same sex. I am not talking of the myth that seduction of an adolescent by a homosexual will make that adolescent homosexual, which is simply not true, unless the adolescent himself is already predisposed in that direction. But if a young child, in the early period of his life when he is still "polymorphous perverse" (that is, sexually responsive to any form of stimulus), over a long period of time is introduced to homosexual outlets by which he gains love and protection and gratification, such learned patterns of gratification may become reinforcd and fixated in such a way as to result in a permanent homosexual pattern. This sometimes happens between a younger and an older brother.

In addition to such familial factors which are probably of great significance, there may also be certain social factors. The process of acculturation takes place not only in the family, but also through peer relationships. We learn a great deal of how to behave, both in a masculine and feminine way, from our peers; and faulty or disturbed peer relationships or the failure to have adequate opportunity for coeducational peer relationships which often occurs with an overprotective, smothering kind of mother figure, or in non-coeducational schools, may facilitate a homosexual pattern.

There are also other idiosyncratic factors such as body build. For example, a girl who, by the standards of our culture, is considered unattractive by her peers, or a boy who is poorly coordinated and unable to function, may very early in their lives be called tomboy or butch, or sissy or fairy, and their resulting sense of isolation and inadequacy may push them toward homosexual adaptation.

It is also important to know that there is no such thing as a homosexual personality: homosexuals vary as widely in their personalities as do heterosexuals, and thus it is as absurd to talk of a homosexual personality as it is to talk of a heterosexual personality. Also, homosexuals differ widely in appearance. As has been pointed out, only a small proportion of male homosexuals are identifiable by female mannerisms. The vast majority of homosexuals cannot be distinguished by their appearance or their speech. This is true for women as well as men. Homosexual men may be extremely masculine in appearance and manner, just as homosexual women may appear outstandingly feminine.

It is true, however, that homosexuals tend to be more promiscuous than heterosexuals. There are a number of reasons for this, some of which probably stem from certain factors that are more common among homosexuals than heterosexuals. There is, for instance, the fear of being tied down, of being overwhelmed in an intimate or stable relationship; also, because homosexual relationships are not legally binding, they are more easily entered into and broken. It is quite possible that if strong, binding cultural factors did not exist in heterosexual relationships, we might have far more widespread promiscuity among heterosexuals as well.

The assumption that homosexuality is, *ipso facto,* an illness *

---

* Note: On December 15, 1973, the Trustees of the American Psychiatric Association voted to discontinue listing homosexuality as a mental disorder in its official nomenclature of mental disorders, and replaced it by a category called "sexual orientation disturbance," "for individuals whose sexual interests are directed primarily toward people of the same sex and who are either disturbed by, in conflict with, or wish to change their sexual orientation." The ruling emphasized that this diagnostic category is distinguished from homosexuality "which by itself does not necessarily constitute a psychiatric disorder." This ruling was ratified on April 8, 1974 by majority vote in writing of the A.P.A. membership.

is one that has been widely circulated, largely (and unfortunately) because the knowledge of homosexuals by most psychiatrists is based almost entirely on those who come to their offices for various emotional and psychiatric disorders that are as common to heterosexuals as to homosexuals. It is only when we move out into the community and begin to study homosexuals in the nonpatient population, *e.g.,* those who are making satisfactory life adjustments, those who live quiet, stable lives as doctors, lawyers, judges, police officers, clergymen, government officials, teachers, sports figures, university professors, social workers, and so on, that we begin to find that the assumption that they are all ill is just another of the stereotypes and myths about homosexuals that are so widespread in our culture.

Many homosexuals are well adjusted with their homosexuality. They have their own community, they are as happy as most of us are. After all, nobody is happy all the time and being heterosexual certainly does not guarantee happiness. Homosexuals have an additional burden to carry, of course, in the sense that they usually feel they have to keep their predilection secret because in societal terms it is looked down upon. But we must remember that people with emotional strength can often sustain such burdens. History is replete with instances of individuals who have tolerated a position or a status which has made them very unpopular with their contemporaries, and yet, because they have been so convinced of the rightness of their stand, they have had the courage to accept themselves and go on living their lives without anxiety.

Obviously, if our societal attitudes toward homosexuality were to change, homosexuals who have self-demeaning feelings of inferiority would probably be fewer in number. In ancient Greece, where homosexuality (really bisexuality) was a highly regarded form of behavior, those men who had bisexual predispositions were held in high esteem by their contemporaries and did not think less of themselves at all. So the attitudes of the system, of the milieu, have a great deal to do with the way a homosexual regards himself.

We know that laws against homosexuality are not effective. There appears to be no greater incidence of homosexuality in countries where consensual sexual behavior between adults in private is not illegal, than there is in societies where it is illegal.

It is important therefore to recognize that (although within the mores of our culture homosexuality is regarded as deviant) homosexuals ought not to be stereotyped as contemptible, nasty individuals, but rather as sexual variants from the norm. Those of them who are able to make a good adjustment with this sexual object choice are entitled to do so as long as they do not force themselves upon unwilling or immature partners, and do not violate ordinary standards of public decency. These same qualifications apply to the behavior of heterosexuals as well. Our ability to look at homosexuals in this way could go a long way toward achieving the kind of humane and civilized society to which we all should be committed.

REFERENCES

Marmor, J. " 'Normal' and 'deviant' sexual behavior." *J.A.M.A.* 217 (1971), pp. 165–170.

Dorner, G. "Tierexperimentelle untersuchungen zur frage einer hormonellen pathogenese der homosexualitet." *Acta Biol. Med. Germ.* 19 (1967), pp. 569–584.

Kinsey, A., Pomeroy, W. and Martin, C. *Sexual Behavior in the Human Male*. Philadelphia, W. B. Saunders, 1948.

Kolodny, R. C., Masters, W. H., *et al*. "Plasma testosterone and semen analysis in male homosexuals." 1971. To be published in *New Eng. Jour. Med.*

Talking About Sex

The Sex Interview in Counseling

Wardell B. Pomeroy *

For twenty years one of my major jobs at the Institute for Sex Research was to interview people and get their sexual histories. The Institute, in total, took about 18,000 histories from all sorts of people across the country. Young and old, rich and poor, black and white, male and female. Of those 18,000 histories, I personally took about 40 per cent. So, in a rather structured interview, I talked to some 8,000 people about what they did sexually. In 1963 I moved from Indiana to New York where, for the last eight years, about 50 per cent of my practice has been marriage counseling in which I see husband and wife jointly. Another 25 per cent has been involved with specific sexual problems and 25 per cent concerned with general psychological problems. While I am not particularly an expert in issues of morality or ethics I have had a good deal of experience in talking to people about sex.

Of course, each therapist works differently. We have our own personalities, our personal needs. So the way I work may be quite different from the way somebody else would work, because we are different people. The best I can do is to tell you how I work, and then you must extrapolate from that anything you feel might be helpful to the way you work.

In marriage counseling, I find that one of the areas I'm work-

* Wardell B. Pomeroy, Ph.D. Psychotherapist, New York, N.Y. Formerly Director of Field Research, Institute for Sex Research, Bloomington, Ind.

ing with more than any other is communication. The way in which a husband and wife are able to talk to each other about anything at all is often a problem. I'm also working constantly with the problem of how I myself communicate with my patients and they with me. Sex, it seems, is a particularly sensitive and difficult subject for most people to communicate about, whether between counselor and patient or between husband and wife, or between any other two individuals.

Eight years ago as I was starting practice in New York, I began to find, for example, that a lot of my patients weren't paying me. I would bill them at the end of the month and they wouldn't pay and I'd bill them the second month—and I found I was getting more and more irritated with them. I would sit there fuming in my chair, as they were telling me about some sexual part of their lives. And suddenly it dawned on me: "Pomeroy, you've got a hangup." It wasn't about sex, because I could talk to them freely and openly and immediately about that. I had a hangup about money! I faced up to this and worked through it until I was able to talk about money to my patients, and then they began to pay me.

I bring this up because I think I can empathize better with those who *do* have troubles in talking about sex with patients or parishioners or counselees because I experienced the same thing, though in a different area.

Gradually, I have come to feel that one of the prime factors in successful sex counseling is the creation of a situation in which unhampered communication about sex can take place. As I talk to my patients and to my research subject about sex, I continually get reactions from them indicating how relieved they are that they can talk to somebody openly and honestly (and without being judged) about their sexual lives. People are asking for this kind of opportunity, of which there are so very few in our inhibited culture. Just being able to talk openly and freely about one's sex life, whether to a minister, a psychiatrist, or even sometimes to a friend, can in itself be tremendously therapeutic.

When a couple come in with a sexual problem that is part of a total marital problem, the first time I usually see them together. Very often I ask them to turn and face each other, and begin to talk to each other about what's troubling them, why they're coming in. This is when I pick up their inability to communicate with each other, as well as some of their gripes and difficulties. Usually during the first hour I will dismiss one and then ask the other, "What else do you want to bring up that you felt you couldn't talk about when your spouse was here?"

Occasionally under these circumstances I get a history of extramarital intercourse. Very often I get, "No, I can tell everything in front of my husband (wife)." Then I dismiss the first partner and have the spouse in to do the same thing. After that first session, I see them individually, usually for two sessions each. During that period of time I get a complete history—not only a sexual history but a social history—from each of them. I explain to them that I need to get to know them better as individuals before we can work conjointly.

Usually, after the two sessions each, I bring them back together and we begin talking again. By that time I have a framework in my mind as to who and what these people are and much more information about what their problems are. Before one can begin to get at feelings and problems with patients, one has to have a certain amount of information about them and know them as people. My own system is to get this information first before I begin to worry about what the problems really are and what's back of them.

A first requirement in creating a climate of communication is to convince patients that what they're telling me is *absolutely* confidential. For example, with a husband and wife the big question is: Am I going to repeat to the spouse what the other is telling me? The way I handle this is to say to them that they're free to tell me anything that they want to and it will remain absolutely confidential, because I've worked with confidences for twenty-eight years and know how to keep them.

I make only two exceptions to this. If one spouse tells me something which I feel is important for the other person to know, and which is not sensitive, not confidential, I explain that I feel free to tell the spouse. On the other hand, if something emerges in such a sensitive area as extramarital intercourse or as feelings about each other that they can't express, and I feel that it would be helpful for the other spouse to know about this, I will say, "I won't ever tell this, but I urge you to tell your spouse about these things."

There is a second factor in creating this climate of communication, however, that I think is by far more important. This is to convince the patient or the counselee that I am not evaluating what they do sexually. I'm not making judgments as to what is right, what is wrong, what is socially desirable or undesirable, what is moral, what is immoral. In this the counselor has to be aware of more than just verbal communication. Such things as a raised eyebrow, a hesitation in the voice, and many other nonverbal expressions also communicate judgments. Patients are very quick to pick up whether you're evaluating what they're saying. I find this to be particularly true of people at lower social levels, who I think are more perceptive than those at upper social levels.

I think that where counselors do have specific judgmental values, it is better to make these explicit to the patient because they're going to be picked up, anyway. But I would urge that the fewer of these you have, the better off you will be in getting the rapport and the empathy with patients that you need.

Now, against this background of the problem of communication in sex counseling, I'd like to detail a few specific suggestions as to how one gets people to talk about sex.

The Counselor as Human Being

Like the person. I think it's important for the counselor to like the person he is talking with. We found in our interviewing of the research subjects—whether they were in back alleys, were psychotic, feebleminded, drunks, drug users, physically filthy, or what not—that the thing to do was to find some saving grace, some favorable asset of this person, and relate to that. It might be a twinkle in his eye, it might be his heartbreaking story, it might be almost anything. If we would find something that we could relate to, we found it much easier to overlook the rest and get to the real data. I would suggest that in general if you don't like people, then you would do better not to try to counsel them.

There can even be occasions when it may seem best to refuse to counsel a particular patient, and to make a referral to another counselor. I once was involved in counseling a very sweet, friendly woman whose husband was one of the most uptight, mean men I have ever run across. He had beaten her up—which I didn't like and I told him so. Finally, I said "Look, this is my feeling toward you. I like your wife and I can work with her. I just can't work with you."

This shook him up a great deal. I had seen him three or four times up to that point, and he said "Give me another chance. Let me come in and see you one more time." That was the turning point of the whole case with him. From then on, I was able to work with him and we ended up being good friends, the three of us, before we were through.

Treat people as equals. I also feel that it is important to treat people as equals. When you're dealing with your own social level this is easy to do. But I've seen too many clinicians, too many counselors, who are condescending, who don't observe the amenities if the person is not of their social level. They call him by his first name and expect to be called "Dr. So-and-So" in return. We found in our history-taking that no matter how mentally handicapped the person was, or how inadequate in any area, he responded favorably when we considered him our equal. It is surprising to see the sort of rapport one can gain by this sort of approach.

Recording the Interview

Maintaining rapport. We found that it was important to do an absolute minimum of recording at the time of the interview. Too much was lost if we did no notetaking at all, but rapport suffered if we spent too much time scribbling copious notes. So we developed a code such that on one sheet of $8\frac{1}{2}'' \times 11''$ paper the equivalent of perhaps twenty-five typewritten pages could be recorded. I still use the code and this means that when I'm talking with a patient, I have off to one side a blank sheet of paper. I may be making dots or dashes or little symbols as we go along, but I'm not getting in the way of the flow between patient and myself. Too many counselors and therapists busy themselves writing down what the person is saying. In my counseling, I have adapted a modification of that same code. I would urge therapists who are doing extensive work to develop a code of their own. It's not too difficult to develop, and the amount of time it can save you is surprising. Also, this means that no one but you can read the record.

Systematic interviewing. This method of coded recording is also helpful in showing at a glance, and during the interview itself, what has been covered and what has not. There is a real need for systematically covering the things you feel are pertinent to the situation. Too often we get involved in some esoteric or unusual part of the patient's life and forget systematically to cover such basic items as masturbation, nocturnal emissions, the use of drugs, or other topics. Then, months later, we may find there are important elements that we've missed. I explain very often to my patients that in doing this, I am closing as well as opening doors. By this I mean that if, let's say, I ask a person, "Have you smoked pot?" and he says, "No, I've never tried pot," I can close that door. We don't have to pursue the subject further. If I ask a patient about his homosexual history and he convinces me that he has none, that door is closed—we can forget it. But if you don't ask the question, you can never close the door. So, in an interview you do two things: you open up avenues of inquiry and therapy, but also you close avenues that are unnecessary to explore further. I feel this becomes important both to the gathering of information from people and to working out a therapeutic relationship with them.

There may be some small risk of forcing the person to deal with a subject before he is ready. But in general, however, it is my view therapists have been far too timid in talking about sex. In most instances their patients are farther ahead of them than they realize.

Flexibility in Structuring the Interview

Fully as important as systematically covering the subject matter of the interview is the ability of the counselor to be flexible in guiding the course of the interview through the various areas it must cover. If he starts off with the most sensitive areas, then he is going to get resistance. As a matter of policy, I start out with completely nonsensitive questions like, "Where were you born? What education have you had? What kinds of work have you done?"

The first sex area I get into is about early sex information: "How old were you when you first learned that the baby grows inside the mother?" This doesn't have many emotional overtones. Then, "When did you first learn about intercourse? First knew it existed?" This is the first opportunity to bring in the word "intercourse." I go through several questions about early sex information. I get the history of their adolescent development—pubic hair, breast growth, voice change in the male, and so on.

Then I go back to early sex experience and preadolescent sex play. "How old were you when you first played doctor?" or when there was any genital play with a boy or a girl. Again, this was when they were very young. They usually don't feel very responsible for this, so it is the next least sensitive area.

From here on, my procedure varies. With the upper-level males, I usually go on to masturbation, and from there to petting, to premarital intercourse, to marital intercourse, to extramarital, and to homosexual behavior. With females, I'll skip masturbation, go directly to petting, then usually to premarital intercourse, marital intercourse, then back to masturbation, and to homosexuality. With lower social level males, I go directly to intercourse, because such information is much easier to get from them than either masturbation or petting. This is generally true of lower social level females as well.

Assume Full Range of Sexual Experience

While it may be wise, in any given situation, to remain flexible as to the sequence in which the nature of the patient's sexual experience is explored, this must always be done against the basic assumption that each patient has had a full range of sexual experience. It isn't a question of: "Did you ever masturbate?" The questions is: "How old were you when you first began masturbation?" And in your marriage: "How often has the masturbation been?" And: "When did you first have extramarital intercourse?" etc., etc. This puts the burden of denial on the persons being interviewed and makes it much easier for them to tell you about it when they assume that you already believe they have because it's such a usual thing. If they haven't, or if it is a direct violation of their value system, they very quickly deny it.

In the long run, it seems clear that we get considerably more information from people when we ask in this way, and, secondly, that we get more positive feedback from people who indicate that they are relieved to feel that we know what it was about.

Within the context of the counseling setting, of course, it is always necessary to recognize possibly equivocal areas. For example, if I am taking the sexual history of a person and get absolutely no clues at all that he has had intercourse with animals, he's never lived on a farm, he has no fantasies about it, I would probably not say, "How old were you the first time?" but "Have you had . . . ?"

There's something of a middle ground here, unquestionably. But certainly so far as the common and usual items like masturbation, premarital intercourse, extramarital intercourse, mouth-genital contact, and so on, are concerned, I would consider it better to assume that they have all been a part of the counselee's experience.

The Vocabulary of the Sex Interview

The problem of the vocabulary of the sex interview requires special attention. While it may pose a special difficulty for the non-professional sex counselor, we all are guilty of employing euphemisms in this area. We've built up a whole system of euphemisms about death, for example, which is bad enough. But when it comes to sex, this is horrendous.

"Have you ever had premarital sex?" *Everybody's* had premarital sex. But that isn't what you're really asking. You're really asking, "Have you had premarital intercourse?" "Have you ever slept with anybody?" You're not interested in how much sleep he gets, and most intercourse isn't involved in sleep, anyway! I think it is very important for the patient to learn that you are not afraid of talking directly and specifically. As soon as you start talking in euphemisms, the patient is going to feel that you aren't sure of the subject, so that you have to talk around it.

A colleague told me of the time when a girl student came in because of a communication problem with her fiancé. She looked so naïve that she triggered all his middle-class stereotypes. When he sought to inquire about the sexual relationship between them, he found himself saying: "Let me just find out, are you sleeping with him?" She said, "No, we've never slept together. We have sex two or three times a week, but we've never slept together." Now, you see, I wouldn't let her get away with that. I'd immediately follow up with, "And does the sex include intercourse?"

If you don't watch yourself carefully, you will find yourself falling into this trap time and time again, not only with your patients but even in your ordinary conversations.

Another aspect of the problem of honest communications centers on the question of the technical terminology used by the counselor. For instance, if you were asking if they had coitus, would you say "Have you had intercourse?" or "Have you had coitus?" or would you alter your terminology somewhat to the more common language that *they* might use? My general policy is that I use the most technical language that they not only know but are comfortable with. And there is a difference. They may know the word "intercourse" for example, but they may not be comfortable with it. "Fucking" may well be more familiar and so you use the word that they are comfortable with. If you have a choice, you use the most technical one you can.

I find myself, particularly in the past, constantly working with these words and finding out what words are the appropriate ones to use. This is true not only of the sexual words but with general language. For example, lower level class people are never "ill," they're "sick." And they've never "injured," they're "hurt." And although they know the word "ill" and know the word "injured," they just aren't comfortable with them. It may take some exploring, but you can establish an amazing rapport when they feel comfortable because you are communicating at their level. Physicians in particular, I feel, have been remiss at this point. They've developed their own technical jargon and in many cases use it as a façade to hide behind so that they *don't* get close to their patients. I think this does nothing but create distance between the two.

Not only are there euphemisms that are used but there are some rather stilted phrases. I've even read reports that spoke about "carnal knowledge" and "sodomy." What is "sodomy"? It has four or five different definitions, so it's better not to use the word. If you're talking about "anal intercourse," talk about "anal intercourse." If you're talking about intercourse between humans and animals, say so. If you're talking about mouth-genital contact, say that.

The matter of vocabulary also becomes important, in a slightly different way, in working with the homosexual group. If somebody comes out with this sort of sentence: "I love to cruise tearooms, but lace curtains through a glory hole make me sick," and you can translate that, you've got a friend. He knows that you know something about the homosexual life. And if you don't know, you ask him to tell you, so that the next time you will know!

But so far as using such words is concerned, my policy is that I don't use them back, unless I'm absolutely sure of what they mean and I feel comfortable in using them. I find, for example, that about 50 per cent of my practice is Jewish, and so I'm trying to learn many of the Jewish words "mishigas," "mikvah," and so on. What *is* a circumcision rite? And what does it *really* mean? What is the significance of the bar mitzvah, and so on? The more I can feel comfortable with using these words, the better I think I can communicate with my patients. So I'm constantly trying to work with language as a means of communication.

Two Problems in Communication

While there is a sense in which the entire counseling process could be considered as an exercise in communication, there are two additional aspects of the problem of communication which deserve at least a brief mention:

Suggesting answers. It's very easy to suggest answers to people. "How often do you have intercourse with your wife?" . . . "Oh, about average." If you then ask, "About two times a week?" this means that you think that's the average he should have and so he gives you the answer you suggested. Notice too that I specify "wife" or "husband" in this question, to pave the way for later questions on extramarital sex.

Actually it is best to suggest a *range* of answers: "How often do you have intercourse with your wife?" . . . "About average." Then I may say, "Well, was it once a month, twice a day, once a week, once a year, three times a week?" I have suggested various answers, but notice that they're randomized, neither in ascending nor descending order. I'm trying to suggest ranges outside his probable behavior. Then it's easier for him to identify his own frequency without floundering around. If you don't suggest some answers well outside of the probable range, you're in trouble, because then he will become too embarrassed to tell you of either a lesser or greater frequency than you have suggested.

Providing assurance. I do a great deal of reassuring when I'm talking with people. "Yes" . . . "Uh-huh" . . . Nodding my head and smiling . . . "Of course" . . . "All right." All of these are reassuring words and actions that help keep the process of communication open. So, when a person says, "I had intercourse with my sister last night," and I say, "Fine," he knows that this doesn't mean fine that you had intercourse with your sister! It means, fine, you're able to tell me that you had intercourse with your sister. Your reassurance is not agreeing with all of their sexual behavior, but is an appreciation of the fact that they're able to talk to you and tell you about it.

Sex Counseling in Other Contexts

Although certain techniques of interviewing people about sex may be helpful, I feel that the overriding factors in successful sex counseling are the ease one feels about one's own sexuality and the acceptance one has for other people's. Without these no amount of correct technique will be useful, and with these, techniques can be easily learned.

The question has been raised as to whether the clergy are in a separate category because they are supposed to reflect the stance of organized religion. I would take a contrary position. When a person of any persuasion (be he psychiatrist, psychologist, social worker, or of the clergy) enters into a therapeutic or counseling dialogue with another person or persons, his aim and responsibility should be that of facilitator and healer. Fear that parishioners will be embarrassed at having contact with their ministers outside the therapeutic relationship reflects, in my mind, only the embarrassment it is anticipated the minister will feel. I believe this is a well-rationalized cop-out that some clergymen use to get them off the hook of their own uncomfortable feelings about sex.

In the past few years medical schools have begun to give courses in human sexuality. Theological seminaries have been slower to develop in this direction. I feel it is imperative that they do so. For those members of the clergy who have not been trained in this area or for those who feel uncomfortable in talking about sex I would suggest they refer parishioners to others who are more comfortable.

Sex is, in our culture, a sensitive and sometimes explosive area. I feel, however, that the lay public can be open and relaxed about it if the counselors are, and that they are begging for the opportunity to open up their hearts and souls to someone who will listen non-judgmentally.

Sexual Knowledge, Attitudes and Values in Three Subcultures

Adolescence

CARLFRED B. BRODERICK *

The researcher who works with college students has one of the easiest jobs in the world. This group is so thoroughly researched that there's scarcely anything they think or feel that somebody hasn't done a thesis on. In contrast there is probably no population in America right now that is harder to get to than the high-school population. With all the troubles school administrators have—raising money through bond issues and the sex education issue over the last five years, for example—letting in a researcher, especially a sex researcher, is something that they're extremely shy of. Accordingly it's very difficult to get permission to ask young people questions.

Perhaps this is as it should be. From the viewpoint of the administrator, it is probably right that such studies should have a rather low priority. But this does mean that the researcher frequently has to deal with much smaller samples than is statistically desirable. And he often must be content with a fairly primitive level of research sophistication. Typically, the data comes from the master's thesis of some graduate student who has finally persuaded the principal in his old alma mater to let him circulate a questionnaire. It therefore follows, unfortunately, that the information available from studies often is not very cannily designed to get at deep things, but rather tends to be simply descriptive.

* Carlfred B. Broderick, Ph.D., Department of Sociology, University of Southern California, Los Angeles, Calif.

The Generation Gap

One of the things that always intrigues people these days is the generation gap. And it is interesting, though probably not surprising, to learn that depending on which way the statistics are developed, it can be shown either that there's an enormous generation gap or that there is none!

To show that there is an enormous generation gap, the researcher should ask questions of young people about their sexual attitudes and behavior and values, and take a mean; he should then ask their parents the same questions, and find and compare the two means. Invariably it will appear that the young people are more liberal in their sexual attitudes than are their parents. The differences are always significant at the .05 or, with a large enough sample, at .01 or still larger .001. The larger the sample the more zeroes before the one.

More sophisticated researchers have found that if people are asked about their sexual values in respect to their *own* behavior and their sexual values with respect to the behavior of a hypothetical child of theirs, they give much more conservative values in the second case. "It's all right for me, but, no, I wouldn't want my daughter or my son to do the same thing." Young people of high-school and college age hold more liberal standards for their own behavior than they say they would hold for their children. Which is only to say, probably, that the role of parent is a conservative and protective one, for no one wants to be responsible for his own children's downfall.

The staff member of the Commission on Obscenity and Pornography faced the same difficulty when he was struggling to find out what the harmfulness of pornography might be. First, he asked his fellow staff members if they thought that handling all the explicit sexual materials had been harmful to *them*. They had seen some fairly raunchy pornography as a part of their work for the Commission and they thought about it and said, "Wel-l-l . . . no. Look, come on. For a middle-aged woman or a man like me life holds very few surprises. I've seen it all before. No, it can't touch me, but, you know, my kids, they're young, they're just newly married. I really don't think it would do *them* any good to see it."

Now, the staff member had children of his own of about that

age, so he went home and asked them if they thought it would hurt them. They said, "Well, let's see what it is and see if it hurts us." So he showed it to them and they said, "That's pretty strong stuff but it doesn't hurt us. After all, we're married and, although we haven't had that much experience, still we can make sense of this. But we don't think you ought to show it to the younger kids— they're only eighteen or nineteen and it would *really* get *them*."

So, researcher to the end, he went on to his teenagers and asked, "Do you think that pornography might really upset your age group?" They said, "Well, like what?" So he showed them some. They said, "Oh, that's not so much, we see that sort of thing. . . ." He said, "Well, do you think it's upsetting or hurtful?" They said, "No, not to kids our age, but now, ten or twelve . . . that would *really* get *them*." The researcher could never find any-body who thought it could hurt him, for the ten- and twelve-year-olds thought that probably four- or five year-olds would be upset, but—and everybody knows nothing upsets four- or five-year-olds. And so everyone is always protecting the next younger age group.

The same seems to be true about sexual attitudes and values: You can put a person in the role of deciding how permissive the next younger age group should be and he's always quite protective, but he's *never* protective of his own age group. So the researcher is never quite sure that the generational differences he discovers represent a genuine change between people born in different eras or whether they are simply a case of people behaving as parents versus people behaving on their own behalf.

But by running correlations instead of comparing averages, it can be shown that there is little gap. That is, if the question is asked, "Are the kids with the most liberal attitudes the children of the *parents* with the most liberal attitudes?" the answer is Yes, on the average. There are always vivid exceptions, but correlational studies do indicate that children who are on the liberal end of the spectrum for their age group are very much more likely to be from parents who are on the liberal end of the spectrum for their age group.

Content of Sex Education

It is revealing, for example, to ask young people and their parents what they think should be taught in sex education and at what age they think it should be taught. You would be amazed at how similar the lists are. My expectation was that the kids would want a lot more information than the parents would want for their kids. Apparently we sold short both the parents and the kids. That is, the parents saw more value in a wider range of materials at earlier ages than many of us would have guessed from the parental rumblings that we heard in the newspapers, and so on. And the kids were more conservative than we would have guessed for them. Especially were they protective of those younger than themselves in terms of at what age these younger ones should be experiencing information in detail about various subjects.

Now, what are some of those various subjects? First, what do kids know about different topics; second, what do they want to know; and third, what are my opinions about what is helpful for them to know?

Happily, there really has been a re-evaluation in the amount of sexual, or at least reproductive, knowledge that children have. The new wave started in my generation. I am forty and at least the girls of my generation saw the Disney film on menstruation. It showed the egg and the sperm and although it was kind of antiseptic, it was educational. In sixth grade I myself chased down a little girl and got hold of her tightly clutched pamphlet full of fascinating pictures of this red lining that was piling up inside the female and then being got rid of monthly. Although it seemed to me an undesirable thing, at least it was part of the world that I acknowledged as being true.

Today, even more than then, our young people are, at least at a superficial level, sophisticated with respect to reproduction. It takes a person with considerable personal pathology, in my judgment, to get to the latter stages of high school and not have a fair concept not only of where babies come from but also the basic physiology of sex.

There are lots of things that can be improved on in that area and I always have fun talking with young people about reproduction and its more fascinating aspects. I inevitably find, however, that the teachers, including the biology teachers, come up afterwards and say, "I wouldn't want the kids to know it, but I didn't know some of that stuff you told us, myself." And yet they've been teaching biology. So I presume, therefore, that some of the more esoteric facts about reproduction that sex educators dredge up can be fascinating to people. For example, in the average ejaculation there are enough sperm that if they were laid head to tail they would reach for eight miles. But having said that doesn't really add very much to the fundamental understanding of reproduction and I suppose one could make an argument that while there's always a lot of challenge for educators to improve people's understanding of the whys and the wherefores of reproduction, at an operational level young people today understand reproduction pretty well, probably as well as they understand how rockets work or how any of the other complex systems that affect their lives work. That is, they don't understand it in detail, but they have the broad outline of it right.

There are some aspects, however, that they don't know nearly enough about. With the exception of a few well-developed programs, kids of this age don't know much about venereal disease. There have been some programs that I'm sure you've heard about in the newspapers that are really very good at giving children the kind of information about venereal disease that will lead them to recognize their own symptoms. It does not change their sexual behavior so far as we are able to discern, but it does often change their prophylactic behavior and that's a plus in anybody's book. When you have good venereal disease education, you increase the number of young people who are willing to refer themselves when they understand that their confidentiality will be respected.

Young people are interested in, but don't know much about, contraception, and what they do know is unreliable. I used to give very full instructions on all the forms of contraception in my marriage courses, including the rhythm method, until I discovered (to my horror) on examinations that about half the class had the rhythm method backward. Some people just block when you start talking about subtracting this many days from this day and a different number from that day. They just blank out, and later, when they try to remember what it is in a real-life sexual situation, they get it all wrong. So now I tell my students that there is a rhythm method and if they want to know more about it they should ask their doctors.

People seem to worry that young people with good contraceptive information will be promiscuous. That may be true in a broad sense, but it seems more likely that people make the contraceptive decision *after* they've made the sexual decision, not before. It probably is not the case that contraceptive information is sexual license, but even if it *were,* it still remains true that knowledge is power to be socially responsible that many young people lack through just *half* understanding. The overwhelming majority of adolescents know that there *is* the Pill, there *are* condoms. That doesn't surprise anybody. But how they work and what precautions should be taken in using them to make them effective, that is what adolescents don't know very much about. On any questionnaire, many of them are reluctant to admit they don't know all about these things, although many other young people are willing to list V.D. and contraceptive information high on their priority lists.

Learning to Deal With Feelings About Sexuality

But what young people rate even higher is finding out about the opposite sex and how they think and feel. A recent article in *Sexual Behavior* consisted of interviews with five or six unmarried single women in their late twenties. They talked, from their perspective, about sex and pickups and singles bars. It was fascinating to read those interviews. Probably relatively few males have ever had an opportunity to get from the female with whom they might be interacting sexually so candid and on the record a discussion of sexual matters.

Certainly, one thing that young people, and the husbands and wives that come for marriage counseling, don't do well is to perceive how the other person feels. Often it's not so much a lack of their perception, as that the other persons have never been very candid about their own feelings—even to themselves.

One of the things that fascinates young people, and challenges those who teach them, is how to get them to express their feelings to each other in a safe way. One reason that males and females don't communicate very well with each other is that they're in a kind of contest system where sexual communication always has an element of negotiation in it. That is, it's rarely the case that male and female in a one-to-one situation can communicate attitudes about sex without social consequences. One would always tend to place an interpretation on any self-revelation in terms of "Well, where is that supposed to lead this relationship? What does that say about whether you want to get in bed with me or not?" Or, "What kind of person do you think I am?" Or, "How easy a lay or how oversexed or undersexed or hung up am I?"

Under those circumstances people are not about to reveal very much of themselves, and what they do reveal will be filtered through their own perception of the kind of an image they want to create with the other. But in the article in *Sexual Behavior,* these women were very candid about some of the sexual myths. For example, they started talking about what a girl wanted from sex versus what a guy wanted from sex, and initially they rehashed the standard party line. They said, "A girl wants a relationship—she wants *meaning* with her sex," and so on. Then one girl said, "You know, that's a lot of bull. Sometimes I want those things, but sometimes I just want some good sex." Then another girl in the group said, "Well, all right. Yes, sometimes. After all what would I be hanging around a singles bar for if I wanted a relationship? Sometimes I really want just a body." Not too many girls say that because it's not culturally acceptable. Girls are supposed to want a relationship and *boys* are supposed to want warm bodies, and then they trade, they exchange, they negotiate, so that both of them get warm bodies *and* relationships and therefore everybody is happy.

Sometimes a woman will acknowledge this late in marriage when she learns to appreciate sex for its own sake, but here was a group of girls talking about both aspects of it and what it meant to them. Not too many men get that kind of discussion going.

After these girls talked about their multiple sexual experiences, one of them asked, "But are there any of us who don't feel guilty about it?" And then they talked about that, and some said, "Well, yes, I feel guilty but I don't feel I *should* feel guilty." Others said, "How can you help but feel guilty when you know what other people think. I grew up in our culture and, admit it, I feel I shouldn't." To read this was a fascinating kind of opportunity for insight. What male ever gets the chance to talk this way with a girl in a one-to-one situation?

Young people can and should be given far richer opportunities, by using skillful discussion leaders, to communicate with each other about sex and sexual attitudes and feelings than they are getting. The Anaheim, Calif., school system has developed a technique called "dialogue-centered teaching," in which the young people talk to each other about their feelings. Myths about what all girls are like and what all guys want (or whatever) cannot be sustained in a setting which provides plenty of opportunity to check them out. There's always somebody there to say, "Bull" and then it becomes necessary to start backing up and saying, "Well . . . you know, if that's bull, then what *is* right?" . . . "I always thought girls, you know." . . . "Well, now you know better. Some girls maybe, not *this* girl."

That's hard to do in a twosome situation where there is the potential of immediate testing of the expressed opinion—or of taking it personally. In a group discussion the girl is protected by the situation and by a sort of covenant among the members that this is a setting where it's safe to talk about these things. The protection may be only partial, but it seems to be adequate to the productivity of the occasion.

The Art of Sexual Decision-Making

Finally the last category of things which are felt and known and thought by high-school-age young people, and which are important for sex educators of every variety, is this: There's not much understanding among people in general, and among young people of this age in particular, about their own dynamics, about their own decision-making, particularly in the context of sexuality. For example, a series of studies was done examining the circumstances under which a guy "grosses out"—that is, when he makes a sexual move that a girl sees as really dumb and offensive and frightening. It quickly became clear that among both the guys and the girls who have had these experiences, there's very *little* understanding— not just in terms of his understanding what the girl felt and her understanding of what he felt—but by each one of why he did what he did. The guys say things like, "She deserved it." . . .

"What do you mean 'She deserved it?' " . . . "Well, you know, here we were. I had picked her up. It was the first time I ever met her. And she necked and petted. I had her pants off. I had my finger up her thing and she was really enjoying it, you know. And then, when I tried to have sex relations with her, she said, "Oh, no, don't do that.' "

"I got so mad, I said, 'What do you mean, "Oh, no," at this point? You *know* this is what we've been building up to all evening!' And she says, 'Oh, no, I don't feel I want to do that.' " And so he feels he's been made a fool of. He's been led down the primrose path and set up, and so he hurts her, maybe. Or he tries to rape her or he pulls off her clothes or he throws her out of the car or, in some way, he demonstrates hostilely and aggressively and sexually to her that she'd better not try that kind of thing with *him* again.

He goes back to his dorm and he tells the guys about it and they say, "That will teach her a lesson." She goes back to her dorm and says, "What's wrong with this guy? What's wrong with him? I was—we were having a good time and then he suddenly got just *wild* and, you know, he wanted to rape me and—hell, men are all alike. They only just want one thing. They don't go along with being warm and responsive and having fun. They've got to go the whole way or nothing for them. Men!"

Each of them not only doesn't understand the other sex, they don't understand themselves very well. They don't understand the dynamics of the interaction they had. And to talk to them about interpersonal negotiation and bargaining and trading for things gives them a new way of understanding their behavior.

It is entirely possible that there are other ways of interpreting the interpersonal interaction, but this is at least a useful way. For example, a guest lecturer was invited to talk about sexual decision-making with three different classes of high-school girls in a home economics program. The person in charge of the program said, "Now, you're really going to enjoy this first group of girls. They're Track A and they're bright and they'll ask a lot of good questions. You'll *really* enjoy talking to them. Now for Group B; well, they're good, wholesome girls and they're not so bright and they won't ask so many good questions, but I'm sure you'll enjoy them because they're such *nice* girls. Then there is Group C. I'm afraid it

won't be much fun for you to talk to Group C. They're the dumb
ones. But you understand if we don't have you talk to Group C,
they'll hear that you talked to the other groups and it will make
them feel bad, so maybe you could find it in your heart to say
something to this group that would, you know, build them up a
little. We'd appreciate it if you'd do this."

What happened, of course, was that the girls in Group A
asked all kinds of bright questions about sexual decision-making in
the abstract, about systems of decision-making, and about abstract
principles of morality. None of them touched anywhere near home
at all—not within a mile of anybody's navel, for example!

In Group B, a few of the girls were beginning to open up a
bit and talk about, "Yes, well, what if you're with a boy and—well,
you know—suppose you are 'one down' in a relationship and you're
not at a bargaining advantage? I mean that happened to a girl
friend of mine."

The dumb girls in Group C were so dumb that they didn't
know any better than to say, "Yeah, I been with a man. That's
what guys do, all right. Then suppose you get pregnant, what do
you do with a baby?"

Another girl in this group said, "I know I'm not too bright,
but, geez, you can't just sit home all the time and. . . ." She said
"jack off," which was perhaps not the most appropriate term, but
apparently she had learned about masturbation from a boy and
"jacking off" was what she knew. Group C was the only group of
the three that had no pretensions and was really able to use the
material immediately and openly in the group in terms of their own
situations. All three groups had exactly the same necessity for
understanding the processes of life that they're involved in—the
social, the psychological processes.

It is a great challenge to educators of every persuasion and
from every point of view to help young people make sense out of
the interactions they take part in. It's a common goal among educators of every kind, in the behavioral sciences certainly, to try
to develop ways of expanding understanding for young people.
Although a lot of young people aren't sophisticated enough to
know that's what they're hungry for, it seems to be the case that
if you feed it to them, they discover how hungry they are for it.
Understanding. It gives them a power over their own behavior that

they didn't have before. For example, Willard Waller developed the "Principle of Least Interest," which is that in any transaction or bargaining situation, the person who is least interested in the relationship controls it. Right? If you're selling a car that you don't want to sell very badly, when somebody wants to buy it from you, you can jack up the price on him because he wants to buy but you don't want to sell all that much. But, on the other hand, if you're just desperate to get rid of this old clunker and he doesn't want to buy very badly, then *he* controls the price because he doesn't care about closing the deal as much as you do, so the price is forced lower and lower.

It's the same in a boy-girl situation. If a boy is crazy about a girl and she's just everything to him, while on her side she thinks he's kind of cute but he does have a big nose, which of them controls the level of intimacy that they have? He might get just wildly passionate, but if she doesn't feel like it, then he has to hold back because he doesn't want to queer the relationship. He has to be good and to respect her standards because he wants her to know that he loves her, and the way he can show that he loves her is by behaving himself.

But if, on the other hand, it's she who is crazy about him, who likes his big nose, and whose idea is that she'll just never run into anybody as exciting or challenging or worth while as he is; and he's the one who merely thinks she's cute but the woods are full of cute girls; then what happens if he should make the same move and try something that she felt was out of line? She'll still feel that maybe that's out of place, but she's a lot slower to insist upon it, because *she* is the one who doesn't want to queer the relationship and he's willing to push a little. She's not in the same boat. She has to think to herself things like, "Well, what am I saving it for if it's not for the man I love?" and the boy is saying things like, "Well, if you love me, show me." It just reverses the roles.

The principle of least interest is a simple idea, easily taught, easily grasped, easily illustrated. And it doesn't stand alone obviously. It's part of a network of ideas. One girl, five years after she had heard a talk on this, wrote that she had seen the speaker's name in the newspaper and it had reminded her of that talk, and she wanted to tell him that this was the most important principle in her life. What she meant was that it had given her a handle for dealing with a critical situation which occurred while she was still unmarried. The young man she was unmarried to was pushing her with a line and she suddenly discovered that she was on the short end of the principle of least interest. It so infuriated her to think that he was taking advantage of his lesser interest in her that she changed her responses. And her change in responses so flustered him that he married her. Now, five years later, she wanted to report that she owed it all to the speaker, who, in turn, was doubly glad she wasn't angry—because you never can tell how things are going to turn out!

It isn't necessary to approve of that particular sequence of events to appreciate the fact that understanding *can* be power in a personal relationship. Power over your own behavior, power to an extent over the other person's behavior. It is an important attitude, feeling, value, with especially important implications for the attitudes, feelings, and values of young people in the adolescent age group.

Black Sexuality

ROBERT STAPLES *

Basic to any adequate understanding of black sexuality is an understanding of the historical development of black life in this country. Before blacks were enslaved in North America, their sexual behavior was under strict family and community control, although Africa is too large a continent to permit the making of sweeping generalizations about sexual behavior there. In some cultures the restraint was so great that it was the custom to tie up the female vagina until marriage, a kind of modified form of chastity belt. In other African societies, some institutionalized forms of premarital sex relations were permitted. Thus, it is not possible to judge whether the African experience provided a strict or a permissive culture, but only that there were many variations in sexual values and behavior, and that all sexual practices were under the control of the kinship group or the community (Frazier, 1961).

When blacks were brought to this country, one of the first things that happened was the breakdown of that community and family control. For instance, while there were over six hundred tribal groupings in Africa, their members were put aboard slave ships without regard to tribal distinctions. Because they came from different and sometimes antagonistic tribal groups, there was no particular respect shown by members of one group for the sexual values of another tribal group. The consequence was the incipient breakdown of all sexual controls. The moral basis for restraint on

---

* Robert Staples, Ph.D., Department of Sociology, Howard University, Washington, D.C.

sexual behavior began to change because of the constant infusion of groups from different tribes that did not respect the sexual values of other tribes.

To talk about sexuality and tribal restraints on sexuality, especially premarital sexuality, essentially is to talk about restraints on the female. Hence, under the slave system black women were left defenseless against the sexual assaults of males, both black and white, on the slave plantations. Having been removed from their cohesive groups in which sexual behavior was controlled before and after marriage, black women could be taken at will by other slaves, by the overseers, by the slavemasters. And of course pressures for premarital sexual behavior were maximized among slaves to whom legal marriages were not permitted. Because there was no one to defend the virginity of female slaves, chastity took on less value than it had for the white female population, especially in the South, where chastity was heavily emphasized for Southern white women (Hernton, 1965).

There was also the influence of religion. Again, while it is difficult to generalize about African religions, it was generally the case that, unlike American society where religious values influence sexual values, in Africa violations of a group's sexual mores were considered to be against individuals and not against God, consequently the influence of religious values on the sexual behavior of blacks was minimal. In the United States, however, the role of black religion has often been more expressive than instrumental, the black churches being more oriented toward allowing members to release tensions from the effects of oppression, racial discrimination, and so on, than toward setting moral standards for their constituencies. This does not mean that black churches have not emphasized moral restraint and encouraged chastity, at least for women, before marriage. It simply means that not as much emphasis has been placed on this as in white churches, and of course blacks have not grown up with the puritanical background of most whites in this country. There are some exceptions in the black community, especially among the middle-class religious, where there is more stress on moral purity before marriage. There are also exceptions in certain fundamentalist sects such as the Seventh-Day Adventists, Jehovah's Witnesses and the Black Muslims. But, all in all, it can be said that the black churches have not played as much of a prohibitory role in premarital and extramarital sexual relations among the black population as have the white churches among whites (Reiss, 1964).

Development of Sexual Attitudes

This brings us to the development of sexual attitudes and knowledge in the black population. We find, first of all, that black children are much more likely to get their sexual education from experience and from their peers than within the family. This may reflect the fact that black parents, although they participate in a great deal of sexual activity, are not aware of what kind of sexual information to impart to their children. It is known, for example, that white children are more likely to learn about menstruation, pregnancy, abortion, and so forth, at an earlier age than nonwhite or black children (Bell, 1968).

Once again, there are some exceptions among the lower-class groups, usually Puerto Ricans and lower-class whites. One study by Rosenberg and Bensman (1968) found, for instance, that blacks have more knowledge about sex at an earlier age than some Puerto Rican and lower-class white groups. Even though blacks are not as knowledgeable about sex at as early an age as are whites, they still have a more heightened awareness of sexual behavior than many other groups. This is a result of certain elements in black culture and other variables that are related to their class location. For instance, the greater socialization by peers leads to a heightened awareness of sex at an early age. Also, the fact that black children become more involved in adult activity, because of the lower-class character of their lives, affects their sexual socialization. They are more likely to live under overcrowded conditions where they can observe sexual behavior at first hand. This they attempt to imitate, thus making an earlier entrance into heterosexual relations than do whites. (Hammond and Ladner, 1969). This does not necessarily involve sexual activity, just male-female interaction. For instance, despite the theories of Freud and some others about the normal psychosexual development of children and when boys should become interested in girls, in many a black neighborhood if you don't have a girl friend by the time you enter the first grade, you are considered to be a confirmed homosexual!

As far as sexual socialization is concerned, although black females are early warned against premarital sexual experience, certain elements in black culture tend to militate against their remaining completely uninvolved in a premarital sexual experience.

Contemporary Sexual Standards

For instance Ira Reiss (1964) found that blacks are more likely to have a permissive premarital sex code than whites. In Reiss' research, which deals with what he terms "permissiveness with affection," "permissiveness without affection," and more restrictive moral standards that require abstinence, he found that blacks were more likely to be permissive—that is, they were more likely to have a standard that permitted intercourse, but at the same time they were more likely to require affection as a basis for that standard. Reiss also found that social forces did not influence black premarital sexual activity or standards as much as they did those of whites. For instance, because the black church has not emphasized premarital chastity as much as has the white church, religion does not influence black attitudes about premarital sex as much as it does among whites. In addition, such other variables as how many times they have been in love, their concept of romantic love, whether they're liberal or conservative, and so on, do not affect permissive black attitudes toward premarital sexual standards to the same extent as they do among whites.

As to sexual behavior itself, some of the published and un-published Kinsey data supports the conclusion that by the age of twenty, 80 per cent of black grammar-school-educated females have engaged in premarital intercourse, compared to only 26 per cent of white females at the same age (Gebhard *et al.*, 1958). The immediate conclusion might be that blacks are more permissive, that they have less self-control. But other unpublished data of the Kinsey Institute point out that whites are far more likely than blacks to engage in masturbation, fantasy and oral-genital sex before marriage (Bell, 1968). Therefore it turns out to be not so much a matter of self-control, but of the form that sexual gratification takes among whites and blacks.

These figures are for white and black females because it is among them that the greatest variations in sexual attitudes and behavior are found. The male response is usually predictable: they will go as far as they are allowed to go by the female, whether white or black.

Additionally, as related to the participation of black males in premarital sexual activity, there is some question as to whether there exists a black male who has not had premarital sexual relations. At least it is difficult to find one who will admit to such a lack. This, of course, reflects the important value attached to premarital sexual activity among black as well as among white males, particularly within the lower-social-class group (Staples, 1972A).

It should also be kept in mind, in talking about the percentage of blacks and the percentage of whites who have engaged in premarital intercourse, that despite the fact that the average black female is more likely to have had premarital intercourse than the average white female, the discussion is still in terms of proportions, not in terms of absolute numbers. There is a much larger *number* of sexually permissive white females in the society and, while it may not be that important, it does not tell us much about the statistical norms concerning the sexual behavior of the white *group,* but in terms of certain other factors, these absolute numbers do have some significance. For instance, in a study on interracial dating, Sebald (1971) found that black males who dated white females were more likely to have premarital sex relations than white males who dated black females. This illustrates not so much the difference in the premarital sexual code, as the fact that there is a much larger number of white females who are more sexually permissive than black females (Day, 1972).

Differences in Social Class and Black Sexual Behavior

Among the forces in black life that are related to the variations in black sexual behavior and attitude, probably the most important are social class differences. The Kinsey group found that, even with the factor of class statistically controlled, blacks were more likely to have had premarital sexual relations at an earlier age than whites (Gebhard *et al.,* 1958).

Reiss found, by using class control, that middle-class blacks had more permissive sexual attitudes than middle-class whites. This is probably true, but it must be remembered that even so these blacks do not constitute what might be called the stable middle-class group such as would be found among whites in the average class in college. There is a great deal of upward social mobility among blacks, which means that most middle-class blacks have come from lower-class backgrounds. In moving from one class to another many individuals retain the sexual values of the social class in which they originated (Staples, 1973B). At the same time, certain psychological studies have shown a great deal of puritanical sexual behavior and attitudes among middle-class blacks, especially females (Kardiner and Ovesey, 1951; Frazier, 1957). So it is difficult to generalize about the effects of social class except that, at this point in time, blacks and whites are not comparable in terms of class membership.

There is also the fact that among the lower-class group, certain characteristics of lower-class life lead to greater involvement in premarital sexual relations. For instance, the employment of the mother as well as of the father frequently leaves the children unsupervised and thus with more opportunities for engaging in sexual activity. There is also the strong sexual orientation of black males, one of the greatest differences between black and white culture.

Certain demographic factors also create pressures on black women. For instance, there are about a million more black women than black men in this society. At the same time there is the tendency for black males strongly to pursue premarital coitus with their dating partners. Unlike many white males, black males do not have a dichotomized world of "good and bad women." Among whites, for instance the good girl is the one with whom you abstain from having sexual relations and whom you eventually marry. And the bad girl is the one with whom you attempt to have sexual relations and may not marry. Among blacks, all females are likely to receive some sort of attempt at sexual relations during the courtship stage. At the same time, they're facing the demographic pressures of a shortage of black males in the dating pool so that, in terms of who is most committed to maintaining a relationship, usually the black female is faced with the decision to engage in premarital sex when requested or not to do so and lose the relationship, with the awareness that if she loses *this* male, there is a considerable shortage of other males out there. So, her alternatives are necessarily limited. It is this kind of social pressure that impinges on the sexual behavior of black women far more influentially than on white women (Staples, 1973C).

Another class factor is that since blacks are an oppressed group in society, with a generally lower-class position, they have less status to lose from participating in premarital sex relations. Consequently, loss of status does not operate so strongly as an inhibiting factor as among whites of equivalent social class.

Stereotypes About Black Sexual Behavior

Despite all these factors, however, there do exist a number of sexual stereotypes about blacks. There is the image of the black male as being sexually superior, with a larger penis size. Once again, unpublished Kinsey data support the conclusion that the majority of both black and white penises are something less than seven inches. So, the assumed difference in penis size (which many people further assume is related to differences in sexual satisfaction for the females) does not actually exist. But it is also true, according to the same data, that three times as many black males as white males have penises larger than seven inches (Bell, 1968).

There is also the sexual stereotype that black women receive greater sexual satisfaction in marriage because of their greater freedom in the enjoyment of sexuality. Although in general this is true, psychotherapists are well aware that there exist many cases of frigidity among black women, especially among the middle-class women. Whatever the level of sexual satisfaction they do experience, it is probably due to the lack of a strongly operative double standard in black society. The fact that black males do not demand that a female be virginal before she can be considered for marriage means that black women enjoy greater freedom from the more rigid sexual double standard of many white males which requires white women to repress all sexual desire until marriage.

But no discussion of these differences in sexual behavior as between blacks and whites must be allowed to obscure the fact that the similarities between the races in various social classes are much greater than the differences among whites between social classes. In one study, when black and white females in the lower and middle class were asked about their attitudes toward a hypothetical premarital pregnancy, it was found that there was a much greater sense of guilt among middle-class black females than among lower-class white females (Staples, 1972C). So, one has to consider the kinds of variations caused by class and, in some cases, region. Another study found that the greatest difference in sexual behavior among women, as reflected in the percentage who had engaged in premarital sex relations, was related to region. Among white females in the South only 12 per cent had premarital sex relations, whereas among white females primarily in California some 72 per cent had engaged in premarital sex relations. This, coincidentally, was a larger percentage than that among the black females in the South (Staples, 1970).

In summary, it may be said that sexual behavior and sexual attitudes are partly a function of culture and partly a function of class and of other elements in the society, and that all of these need greater investigation before continuing acceptance is allowed to some of the sexual stereotypes that exist today.

REFERENCES

Bell, Allan. "Black Sexuality: Fact and Fancy." A paper presented to *Focus: Black America Series*. Indiana University, Bloomington, Indiana, 1968.

Bell, Robert. "Comparative Attitudes About Marital Sex Among Negro Women in the United States, Great Britain and Trinidad." *Journal of Comparative Family Studies* I (Autumn, 1970), pp. 71–81.

Broderick, Carlfred. "Social Heterosexual Development Among Urban Negroes and Whites." *Journal of Marriage and the Family* 72 (May, 1965), pp. 200–203.

Brown, Thomas Edwards. "Sex Education and Life in the Negro Ghetto." *Pastoral Psychology*. May, 1968.

Day, Beth. *Sexual Life Between Blacks and Whites*. New York: World, 1972.

DeRachewitz, Boris. *Black Eros*. New York: Lyle-Stuart, 1964.

Frazier, Franklin E. *Black Bourgeoisie*. New York: Collier Books, 1957.

Frazier, Franklin E. "Sex Life of the African and American Negro." In *The Encyclopedia of Sexual Behavior*, Albert Ellis and Albert Arbarnel, eds. New York: Hawthorn Books, 1961, pp. 769–775.

Hammond, Boone and Joyce Ladner. "Socialization into Sexual Behavior in a Negro Slum Ghetto." In *The Individual, Sex and Society*, Carlfred Broderick and Jessie Barnard, eds. Baltimore: The John Hopkins Press, 1969, pp. 41–52.

Hernton, Calvin. *Sex and Racism in America*. New York: Doubleday and Company, 1965.

Kardiner, Abram and Lionel Ovesey. *The Mark of Oppression*. New York: W. W. Norton and Company, Inc. 1951.

Ladner, Joyce. *Tomorrow's Tomorrow: The Black Woman.* Garden City, N.Y.: Doubleday, 1971.

Marshall, Donald and Robert Suggs. *Human Sexual Behavior: Variations in the Ethnographic Spectrum.* New York: Basic Books, 1971.

Poussaint, Alvin. "Blacks and the Sexual Revolution." *Ebony* (October, 1971), pp. 112–122.

Poussaint, Alvin. "Sex and the Black Male." *Ebony* (August, 1972), pp. 114–122.

Rainwater, Lee. "Some Aspects of Lower-Class Sexual Behavior." *Journal of Social Issues* 22 (April, 1966), pp. 96–108.

Reiss, Ira. "Premarital Sexual Permissiveness Among Negroes and Whites." *American Sociologist Review* 29 (October, 1964), pp. 688–698.

Rosenberg, Bernard and Joseph Bensman. "Sexual Patterns in Three Ethnic Subcultures of an American Underclass." *Annals of the American Academy of Political and Social Science.* (March, 1968), pp. 61–75.

Staples, Robert. "A Study of the Influence of Liberal–Conservative Attitudes on the Premarital Sexual Standards of Different Racial, Sex-Role and Social Class Groupings." Ph.D. dissertation, University of Minnesota, 1970.

Staples, Robert. "Research on Black Sexuality: Its Implications for Family Life, Education, and Public Policy." *The Family Coordinator* 21 (April, 1972 B), pp. 183–188.

Staples, Robert. *The Black Family: Essays and Studies.* Belmont, Calif.: Wadsworth Publishing Company, 1971.

Staples, Robert. "The Influence of Race on Reactions to a Hypothetical Premarital Pregnancy." *Journal of Social and Behavioral Science* (Spring 1972 C), pp. 32–35.

Staples, Robert. "The Sexuality of Black Women." *Sexual Behavior* (June 1972 A), pp. 4–17.

Staples, Robert. *The Black Woman in America.* Chicago: Nelson-Hall, 1973 A.

Staples, Robert. "Sex and the Black Middle-Class." *Ebony* (August, 1973 B), pp. 106–114.

Staples, Robert. "The Black Dating Game." *Essence* (October, 1973 C) pp. 40, 92–96.

Sutker, Patricia and Richie S. Gilliard. "Personal Sexual Attitudes and Behavior in Blacks and Whites." *Psychological Reports* 27 (December, 1970), pp. 753–754.

Williams, Leon. "Sex, Racism and Social Work." In *Human Sexuality and Social Work,* Harvey Gochros and Leroy Schultz, eds. New York: Association Press, 1972, pp. 75–82.

Zelnik, Melvin and John Kantner. "Sexuality, Contraception and Pregnancy Among Young Unwed Females in the United States." A paper prepared for the Commission on Population Growth and the American Future (July, 1972).

The College Subculture

Lorna J. Sarrel & Philip M. Sarrel *

Our basic knowledge about student attitudes and behavior comes primarily from Yale, but also from Brown, Smith and Mount Holyoke, from Amherst and Southern Connecticut State College, and from the University of Bridgeport. There are some differences between state universities and the Ivy League schools, but not too many, just as there are some differences between the college and the high-school students.

The Yale Sex Counseling Program

Our work at Yale began when Yale became coeducational at the undergraduate level. It consists of three parts:

I. *The course in human sexuality* was originally developed at Mount Holyoke College with Mount Holyoke and Amherst students. It is a noncredit evening course which runs for seven or eight weeks, with a weekly lecture about some aspect of human sexuality after which the class divides into small discussion groups led by trained student leaders rather than by faculty or professional people. The sexuality course is given at Yale once a year, and adaptations of it are also offered at other schools, including Brown, Williams, Smith, and the University of Bridgeport.

* Lorna J. Sarrel, M.S.W., Consultant in Sex Problems, Yale University, New Haven, Conn. & Philip M. Sarrel, M.D., Assistant Professor, Obstetrics and Gynecology, Yale University, New Haven, Conn.

II. *The Yale Student Committee on Human Sexuality* which helped to organize the course at Yale wrote a book called *Sex and the Yale Student,** which has since been given to every incoming freshman. The book discusses what students feel other students need to know about sex. Besides information on contraception, abortion, interpersonal relationships, and so on, it also provides telephone numbers and descriptions of various sex-related health services on the campus.

III. *The Sex Counseling Service* functions within the Student Health Service's Department of Mental Hygiene. We are available every morning of the week. The service is described in *Sex and the Yale Student* as follows:

"Problems and Questions Relating to Sex. For example, sex dysfunction, contraceptions, abortion, pregnancy, sexual assault, etc., are appropriate issues for the Sex Counseling Service. This program remains a part of the Mental Hygiene Division and has in no way changed its policies of separate records and absolute confidentiality."

The book *Sex and Yale Student* was first printed in 1971, at which time it was given to the 9,300 students at Yale and to about 700 members of the faculty who requested it. The initial printing of 10,000 copies disappeared very fast! The costs of the book were borne by the students, who pay a token fee of five dollars to take the course in Human Sexuality. That money creates a budget for the Student Committee on Human Sexuality and since the course includes as many as 1,200 to 1,300 students in a given semester, there is enough money to do such things as printing and making available a book for every student on campus.

Distribution of the book at the time of registration, *plus* the course in Human Sexuality, *plus* the counseling program, constitute what we think of as the foundations of our program of Human Sexuality. There are other components, including a special discussion series for freshmen students and a student-to-student sex counseling program which is supervised by members of the faculty.

---

* An expanded version called *The Student Guide to Sex on Campus* has since been published by the New American Library in soft-cover.

Scope and Changing Emphases

In the first two years of our program, we saw 1,000 students, including 600 of the 800 women undergraduates. So there were very few people we did not see! In the present junior class, who were freshmen when we were "freshmen," there are 225 girls, of whom we've seen 208 on a purely voluntary basis—that is, who have accepted the opportunity to come and talk, to ask their questions, and to air their concerns.

The program has expanded each year, so that this third year we work every morning and some afternoons, but we are still running six to seven weeks behind in appointments by the end of the first week of the semester. Besides these half-hour appointments, several hours each week are set aside for more prolonged discussion, and we also have a policy of seeing everybody for return appointments, regardless of what the presenting issue was.

In our first year about 80 per cent of the students came to us for contraception. That figure has steadily dropped, while the number who come just to talk has increased greatly. This is due partly to a change in our image. For example, men now come to talk to us about their concerns with homosexuality and/or sexual response—cases which we encountered rarely in the first year. We've come to feel that a request for contraception is never a simple one, so we provide a half-hour appointment rather than the usual gynecologic appointment time of fifteen minutes. This allows more time for just talking and, if necessary, we can even stretch it to forty minutes by borrowing a little time from another student who can be served more simply and quickly.

The students need, and want, to talk about a great many questions: Should I/we have intercourse?" . . . "Should I tell my parents that I'm going on the Pill?" . . . "What will this mean to my parents if I do tell them?" . . . "Will this hurt them?" . . . "How will they react?" We believe it is quite valuable for students who need help in thinking through such questions to have someone to whom they can turn. It is for many of them the first time they will make a major decision on their own and do something very important in their lives that they are *not* going to share with their families. It is particularly hard for those students who are close to their parents to make a decision to keep something important from them. These are the kinds of issues they want to talk over with us.

Over half the students who came to us for contraception in the first- and second-year classes had never had intercourse. We were actually seeing as many males who had never had intercourse as females. They were coming to us as couples with the prevailing value on the campus being very simply that you can talk about a decision to have intercourse, you can go to a resource to reflect on this and to obtain contraception, but it is certainly wrong to have intercourse without contraception.

Relationships More Basic Than Sex

The fact that over half of the students we saw had never had intercourse does not mean that they had not slept together! As a matter of fact, we have learned that most student couples pass through several stages of intimacy before engaging in sexual intercourse. Occasionally we get a student who calls with an emergency. One male student came in last year with the book in his hand on such a visit. When we asked what the emergency was, he said that he and his girl friend had decided to have intercourse. When it was pointed out that many people decide to have intercourse without regarding it as an emergency, he said, "Well, but it says here in the book that if you decide to have intercourse, you should go talk to the Sarrels about it, and we're going to have intercourse *tonight,* so it's an emergency!"

When students come to us we usually ask, "You made this appointment six weeks ago. When you made the appointment, what did you want to discuss?" And they'll say very simply, "We decided six weeks ago that we were ready to have intercourse. We've known each other for a period of time. We feel that we have a relationship going where it would be appropriate. We would not have intercourse without contraception and we wanted to come and talk to you about that and about other aspects of first intercourse, about sexual response."

And we'll ask, "Well, do you sleep together?" "Of course we sleep together. We've slept together for a year and a half." Or, "We've been sleeping together since shortly before that decision was made." And they really mean *sleep together* and it is a *very* important stage of a developing relationship. They have continued just to sleep together for that five or six weeks or so while they were waiting to see us. Part of it, then, is a matter of tuning in to the generation and what *their* values are, what *they* feel is important, and also of seeing the kinds of relationships that come through.

Impact of the Sex Counseling Program on Campus Life

It's very unusual for us to see a pregnancy. In our first year, indeed, we saw about the same proportion of undergraduate pregnancies as at other schools. In a number of schools in New England, about one in every six girls will become pregnant while in college. One of the Ivy League schools last year had four hundred undergraduate girls become pregnant. Another school with a much smaller student body had eighty-five pregnancies. We had *five* undergraduate pregnancies in 1971! The year before, of course, there had been more. But when you're seeing half the students before they have intercourse, then you don't have very many pregnancies. Out of the five pregnancies, one was a girl with an I.U.D. and two were girls who had used diaphragms.

It is our belief that this kind of responsible attitude toward intercourse at Yale is directly related to the Sex Counseling Program. Last year, in a clinic in which medical and nursing students saw students from other college campuses, one girl after another came in with the same story, "I've been having intercourse for six months and I've never used any contraception." And, "I've been having intercourse for a year and a half and always used the rhythm method." Our contact with the Yale experience has made us feel that one can have a significant impact on the way young people will deal with their sexual relations. They won't excuse themselves by saying, "We got carried away." Rather, the whole thing becomes a decision-making, rational process in which they think through, in advance, the meaning to them and to their relationship of using contraception.

One thing that we do know about other campuses is that their rates of intercourse are much the same as ours. When comparing a girl's school with a coed school and with Yale, you find that in one school, 46.7 per cent of the girls have had intercourse, in another 47.3 per cent, in another 47.6 per cent. It's all within a half a percentage point no matter what the setting. The only difference is that in the one setting you have an entire student body responding to an educational program. There is the impact of the book, of the course in sexuality, and of the sex counseling services—a tripartite influence that touches almost every student. What we are saying, then, is this: if you direct your attention to being open and honest and making human sexuality a part of the system, you don't *increase* behavior. Behavior is the same. What you do is to affect positively the quality and responsibility of behavior and relationships involved.

Most schools are amazed to hear our figures about venereal disease. We make a gynecological examination of all our female patients, and in our two years of experience we have seen three cases of gonorrhea in a population of 1,000 women. That's extremely low in a country faced with an epidemic of venereal disease. It might be suspected that these students are all cloistered or they're not all involved in a way in which they could get a venereal disease. But we know that's not so. What we also know is that we see very little promiscuity among the Yale students. There may be a preselection factor, but we think we can document it in terms of one-to-one relationships. Also, we've been able to follow a number of students for three years and we know the quality of these relationships. Built into the relationships are the various factors which apparently preclude promiscuity, venereal disease, and the problem of pregnancy.

Nature of Student Decisions

We do not often see couples who ask us for a moral decision, but whenever a girl or a guy, or a couple, comes to us and says, "We want to know whether we should have intercourse or not?" our antennae go up. Just the fact that they've come and asked the question in this way indicates a certain amount of conflict on the part of one or both.

In such a situation we always say, "Well, we're not going to tell you what you should do, but let's talk about it." It's really amazing how much you need to individualize what is going on. There was one couple who came to talk about this toward the end of their freshman year. Should they or should they not have intercourse? It was an excellent relationship. A very loving, long-term one, in the context of a great deal of sexual intimacy, which was very fine for them. Thus there would seem to be no reason why they should not have intercourse.

But they raised such issues as lack of privacy. Now one might say, "Well, how important is that?" But we felt that it was an extremely important issue, that they should not risk having their first intercourse situation in a room where a roommate might come in at any point, where they would feel hurried, where they would feel nervous and anxious about the setting.

Another girl, who came to talk about whether she should have intercourse or not, had found that in petting with her boy friend she had panicked. She had become overwhelmingly frightened about nudity. She had continued a petting relationship, but had to have some underclothing on. She talked a lot about her mother and her mother's standards and what her mother would think, and should she or shouldn't she. In this instance, we felt it was really important to suggest to the girl that she consider discussing it with her mother. What did her mother really believe? What were her mother's standards?

The follow-up is interesting. She did go home at spring vacation and talk with her mother, whose reaction was, "I trust you to make the right decision. I know that I've given you a good sense of what's right and wrong and I feel that you can make this decision." The girl said to us, "When my mother said that without saying either 'You can't or you must not,' suddenly I felt free to decide *not* to!" And she did decide not to have intercourse at that point in her life—a major decision for her. Afterwards, she no longer had the panic reaction in the petting situation—which indicates that her panic had really centered on the unmade decision of whether or not to have intercourse.

Another major issue that students have to face is the double standard. Is intercourse all right for men and not all right for women? At Yale we have six men for every woman—so, given that ratio, almost every woman is involved in a one-to-one relationship. Contrary to the expectations of some, she does not choose to have six. She chooses to have one. Women find it almost impossible to be free-floating in such a situation. There is too much tension, too much pressure. It is too diverting from the basic reason why they came to Yale; namely, to be a student, not to get a husband.

At Mount Holyoke in 1967, the statistics showed that 75 per cent of the girls married within eighteen months of graduation. But these Yale women students go on to medical or divinity or law school, and their reaction to the Holyoke 1967 figures is: "This is absolutely inappropriate. Seventy-five per cent of us are going to marry in eighteen months? You're crazy! Not us. That was women four years ago. Today we're going to be doctors, I'm going to be the first woman Supreme Court Justice of the United States," and so forth. These are today's women.

Although their relationships are one-to-one relationships, ongoing relationships in which fidelity is a highly important factor, they are not likely to be permanent relationships, and it's a mistake to think that they are. The more important factor for the women we're seeing is the woman herself and what she is going to be able to do with her life. When it comes to the question of the double standard, we're faced with some very interesting data. First of all, more women at Yale have had intercourse than have men! By the time they graduate, 62 per cent of the men have had intercourse as compared with 75 per cent of the women. Now that's quite a change from the time of entry as freshmen, when 25 per cent of the women had intercourse and 33 per cent of the men. These data are based on 1,200 students studied in one year.

Also, more women than men feel that men should have premarital intercourse. The men appear to be moving toward looking upon intercourse not as something to be casual about but as something that you really have to think and make decisions about. Also, sex out of the context of a relationship has become a "nono." Thirteen years ago, Amherst data showed that 25 per cent of all male graduates had had a prostitute experience. Today the figure is less than 2 per cent among the Yale *and* among the Amherst students, showing that sex just for the sake of putting a penis in a vagina is something that's out, but sex within a relationship has become an important value for the men.

There is a marked difference between what students feel is the image other people have about sex on campus, and the reality they know. The scene is not a wild, promiscuous one. It's a scene of individual values, of protecting others from being hurt, of people looking after each other in meaningful ways and, we find, relating openly and honestly.

The Nature of Student Pressures

These statistics were eye-openers for us. Learning that 25 per cent of the girls arrived on campus having had intercourse meant that 75 per cent had not. By the end of their freshman year, the number of girls who had had intercourse approached 75 per cent, so freshman year is quite a year for at least half of the girls on campus! These girls come from diverse backgrounds, in many of which premarital intercourse was specifically prohibited. More come from backgrounds in which sex simply wasn't discussed, where you were supposed somehow to pick the standards out of the air. We began to be concerned about the fact that both women and men were subject to pressures to have sexual experience and that some were doing this too soon and without thinking it through. So we started special programs for freshmen to give them an opportunity to talk with older students, to talk with us, to get information, to stand back a bit from this overwhelming campus scene and say, "Well, what really is happening here?"

A girl finding herself living with two other girls both of whom are on the Pill, whose pills are right out in the open and who talk very freely about their sex experiences, feels a not so subtle pressure: everyone does it, you're hung up if you don't. And we wanted to make these pressures explicit so that the realization that they exist can be part of the student's decision-making process. Because if you only feel them but don't realize they *are* pressures, then you may not act in your own best interests.

Another example of the way pressure is exerted upon students and the ways in which they come in to see us is the question of masturbation. We see students now who ask "What's wrong with me, I don't masturbate? Everybody obviously does. Why don't I?" Now we know statistically that 10 per cent of the male students have never masturbated. That means there are 900 to 1,000 males on the campus who have not masturbated. Unfortunately, there does exist a belief, even among doctors, that if a male does not masturbate there's something wrong with him—he has a "low sex drive" or he's really "freakish." That's just not so—not if our data and experience are valid.

But we also see women who come to us saying, "What's wrong with me? I don't masturbate." Or this may come out in an interview. A couple will be talking to us and the girl will ask a question about masturbation and we'll say "Well, do you ever masturbate?" And she'll say "No!" and the boy friend will be very surprised, "Really? I thought all girls did! You don't?"

When we took histories, we found that a third of the girls had masturbated. These were the same figures Kinsey had reported, so there had been no change in the twenty-year interval. Of the two-thirds of the girls who had not masturbated, many did not know what it was. In that third who had were a number who had done so without realizing what it was. There were also quite a number who had experienced an orgasmic response without realizing what it was.

We try to make ourselves available to our students seven days a week and twenty-four hours a day. They know how to get in touch with us by telephone at home and they do. We encourage students to do that, and to come to see us as couples because we feel it's appropriate for their culture to do so. Other resources for students are reading materials and the lecture series on tapes. We put these tapes in the language laboratory and said, "Anyone who wants to can come in and listen to them." In one semester, 300 students came in, pushed the button and listened because they wanted to on their own rather than in the setting of the course.

We also offer the Masters-Johnson type of therapy for students as well as for the general community. Students are concerned about and experience the whole gamut of sexual dysfunctions such as premature ejaculation, ejaculatory incompetence or impotence in the males, and dislike of any sexual contact, non-orgasmic response, and pain with intercourse in the females.

This underscores the importance of sex education for this group, because, for example, the male may become concerned about premature ejaculation even when it occurs in a developmentally normal context. Then, if he identifies himself as having a problem of sexual inadequacy and becomes anxious about it, he definitely *will* have a problem! So it's really important preventive medicine for students who are involved in sex to understand what the facts of sexual function are. For example, we've seen only 6 out of 1,000 women who had an orgasm the first time they had intercourse. That's a pretty important figure to know, especially if you've always assumed that every woman experiences orgasm from the beginning, and you've spent three years of your life faking it and don't know how to tell your partner! Similarly, we know that given a period of abstinence, *all* men are premature ejaculators. For the average college student, just to know that fact is vital, instead of his thinking, "I'm the only one on the Yale campus who comes too fast."

Help for the Homosexual Student

The attitude of the Sex Counseling Program toward the homosexual student deserves particular notice. In the Yale book, there is a description of the programs available for homosexual students. For two years now, the campus ministry has run a program every Thursday night for homosexual students with an attendance of anywhere from 75 to 125 students each time. We feel there must be a place for the student who is interested in the subject of homosexuality or who is homosexual and wants to come and talk about it. In addition, we make quite clear that students are free to bring all such questions into our setting. The highly respected Mental Hygiene Division at Yale is a part of the regular training program for the eight resident fellows in psychiatry. There is a full-time staff of ten people from a variety of disciplines, including psychiatry, psychology, marriage counseling, and social work. The Division serves 1,300 undergraduate and graduate students and student spouses each year and has done so for many years. Thus there are a multitude of resources to which the homosexual student can turn. There is the section on homosexuality in the book *Sex and the Yale Student.* In the book that was its outgrowth, *A Student Guide to Sex on Campus,* there is a whole section on homosexuality written by two homosexual students.

The reception a homosexual male or female gets in the Psychiatry Department undoubtedly is important. He or she would never get the feeling that if they go in and say, "I'm homosexual," they're going to be greeted with "Okay, what can we do to change that?" If they want to try to change their sexual orientation, then the psychiatrist will work with them. But if they are perfectly happy with their sex object choice, that is fine also. The psychiatrist will ask, "How can I be of help to you? Can I help you with adjusting to being homosexual? Can I help you with the problem of whether you should tell your parents?" This problem of how to break it to their families is the number-one concern of homosexual college students. This is where the campus ministry has been of great help, from the feedback that we get. The ministry has also established a trust setting where people can come and talk.

Effects of the Program on Long-Term Relationships

One of the issues on which we do not yet have any real data, of course, is the possible consequences of these campus relationships in subsequent years, in terms of other life relationships, marriage, adjustment to life, and so on. What we have seen is a development of very intimate, living together relationships, honest, open, and for all intents and purposes permanent except that it is without a certificate that says married couple. There is an understanding, however, that at the time it comes to an end, they can end it.

We're not impressed by the fact that there are many relationships breaking up. We've been able to follow a fairly large number through two years of college life from the time they were freshmen or sophomores, and in that period of time the "divorce" rate among these relationships has been far less than the national divorce rate. Whether or not these relationships will continue, it is much too early to say. Other preliminary data indicate, however, that the majority probably will go into permanent relationships. As a matter of fact, we see a great deal of evidence which leads us to believe we are observing a real growth in tenderness, concern and responsibility. Just the fact that students come to us as couples bears witness to this. It's not just a girl or a guy coming for contraception. They're both very much concerned . . . in fact we often get such questions from the males as, "Isn't there something *we* can do? It isn't fair that the girl has to take all of this responsibility. Isn't there a male Pill I can take?"

We would guess that the change among males may be more dramatic than the change among females. The image of the "big man on campus," the guy who bragged about his sexual exploits, the kind of promiscuous male image that we had not too long ago, we just don't see any more. In fact, there are many negative sanctions among the peer groups for the promiscuous—whether male, female, heterosexual or homosexual. There's much emphasis on the importance of a relationship, on honesty, openness and communication. We think this is highly favorable. In turn, it is hard to believe that a nonpermanent relationship built on that kind of foundation is going to be harmful to a later marriage relationship. For this working at a relationship, at the capacity to care for, understand and be concerned for another person, even if it is not permanent, is, at the very least, a good rehearsal for marriage.

The students are primarily concerned with not hurting someone else, especially the someones they are close to. And, as we have learned from Dr. Masters and Mrs. Johnson, the basis of therapy in working with a couple is to keep people from hurting each other. Married couples are always hurting each other without realizing it. This happens because the people involved don't really know each other. We are not nearly so apt to hurt a person we know. The way we come to know is through communication, through very honest expression of feelings, accepting feelings as facts and being able to say, "I feel, I am, I want, I need."

What we see among the students is just this openness of relationship. When two people have this kind of openness with each other they *know* each other; whereas when they don't know each other they can hurt each other. Then eventually hurt leads to anger and frustration and a blowup.

We feel it is important to bring the students to a level where they're not playing childish games any more, but instead are really telling it like it is. They have the freedom of saying how they feel, of not being boxed in. When we're talking about first intercourse, for instance, that certainly should be the setting in which a couple *must* be able to say how they feel, to stop at any time that they want, and to have that trust with the other. If the man is afraid that he is hurting her, he can say so. "I feel the need to know how you feel." That's the message that we give when they ask, "What do you need to know about first intercourse?"

Actually, they are building a relationship of trust. We use the word *vulnerability,* meaning simply "a setting in which one individual can bare his/her innards to the other and not be afraid that the other will put in a knife." We see so many husbands and wives who have never built that trust between each other and who are constantly keeping their innards hidden—the kind of situation

when people come for sex therapy, in which neither knows where
the other is. They've never learned or been helped to learn how
to seize every opportunity to establish trust, and then have their
sexuality unfold in a setting of trust and vulnerability. And that's
the whole therapy: simply establishing that setting. Well, our students are doing just that. They're almost light years ahead of where
our generation was, and out of that comes an enlarged capacity for
tenderness and loving on a very meaningful level.

Sexual Responsiveness

The Role of Religion in
Sexual Dysfunction

WILLIAM H. MASTERS & VIRGINIA E. JOHNSON *

About the only thing which can be said with certainty about human sexual functioning is that we still don't know anything about
human sexual functioning! It remains unequivocally the last great
unexplored field, not only in the profession of medicine but in
the social sciences as well. For even to this date our culture has
not permitted clear exploration of human sexual functioning.
We're still on the fringes. In fact, it can be said with certainty
that we don't even know what we don't know on the subject!

In medicine, if there is an unexplained problem one generally starts in the laboratory, and if anything develops there that
might have clinical application it is integrated into practice. Once
some real degree of effectiveness has been developed in the realm
of therapy, attention eventually becomes directed primarily toward prevention.

While a good bit is now known about what actually happens
physiologically in the realm of human sexuality (and we have
developed concepts of some ways and means of treating sexual
dysfunction with a reasonable return) no one yet has really moved
into the area of prevention of sexual dysfunction. The one exception to this is the work of SIECUS. While the dissemination
of accurate information is obviously one of the first steps in the

* William H. Masters, M.D., Director, Reproductive Biology Research
Foundation, St. Louis, Mo. and Virginia E. Johnson, Assistant Director,
Reproductive Biology Research Foundation, St. Louis, Mo.

prevention of sexual dysfunction, the fact remains that accurate information alone is not the answer to the treatment of sexual dysfunction, much less its prevention. It is a factor, to be sure, but relatively a minor one.

It is to be hoped that this situation is only temporary. The time will surely come when there will be sufficient knowledge and materials to educate with, and a sufficient number of reasonably effective educationalists who are comfortable with the subject. The time is rapidly coming when there will be in the professional population a sufficiently large group of individuals who can accept the concept of the need for wide dissemination of effective information about human sexuality.

Where do we go from there? How then do we move to the *prevention* of sexual dysfunction?

Sex as a Natural Function

The first and the greatest single step to the prevention of sexual dysfunction would be the acceptance by professionals and laity alike of the concept that sex is a natural function. The ability to accept this concept is a measure of how possible it may be to develop an adequate program of prevention in the realm of human sexual dysfunction. And it has particular bearing on the development of an understanding which can afford relief from some of the sexual distresses that relate to religious orthodoxy.

The statement that sex is a natural function is deceptively simple, for there probably is no therapist anywhere who has entirely succeeded in treating sex as a natural function. In terms of definition, what does this really mean? At least for the purpose of definition, a natural function is one that is genetically determined. For example, any obstetrician can remember innumerable instances when the resuscitation and/or initial respiratory stimulation of an infant was his immediate responsibility. Most of the time he won, but sometimes he lost the battle. The one thing, however, that he did not and could not do was to teach the baby to breathe. He may have cleaned out a nasal passage and performed some other normal or emergency routine, but either that infant was able to breathe on the basis of its own innate capacity, genetically determined, or it was not. Neither did he teach that youngster to void or to move its bowels. Nor, if it was a boy, did he teach him to have an erection in the first twenty-four hours of life: he *had* it—in fact, sometimes even before the cord was cut! Achieving an erection is not something anyone is *ever* taught to accomplish. Nor did he teach the girl baby to achieve vaginal lubrication in the first twenty-four hours of her life—it simply happened.

Now, if the sexual function can be conceived of as a natural function, how does this apply to our concerns here? Every natural function has its own uniquely characteristic and specific period of voluntary delay. For instance, it is possible to hold one's breath, but not for very long. One can delay one's bladder function, but not usually for as long as one's bowel function. Each function has its own periodicity of voluntary delay. But sex is unique in this respect, for if the respiratory function is at the immediacy end of the delay spectrum, sexual functioning is at the opposite end of the spectrum. It can be voluntarily delayed indefinitely, even denied for a lifetime, without threat to life.

But the facility to deny sex as a natural function is at the conscious level, and it is at the unconscious level that control slips. Even though one's physical sexual function may consciously be denied, those who are males have erections every sixty to eighty minutes during sleep, and those who are females (although this has not been reported) experience vaginal lubrication every sixty to eighty minutes during sleep.

Development of Sexual Dysfunction

Now, if the concept of sexual response as a natural function can be accepted, at least for the purposes of discussion, then it becomes possible to explore how it is that religion can play a definitive role in the development of sexual dysfunction. This has to do with the long or indefinite voluntary control period. In *Human Sexual Inadequacy,* the point was made on several occasions that in the histories of many individuals referred for treatment, religious orthodoxy had apparently played a significant role in the development of sexual dysfunction. It did not seem to matter whether the orthodoxy was Jewish, Catholic or Protestant.

Nor, indeed, was it even a question of religious orthodoxy *per se*. What made the difference was the patient's interpretation of that orthodoxy. Which is quite another matter.

In terms of sexual functioning, "thou shalt nots" appear to be inevitable to orthodoxy regardless of its source, and are applicable because sexual functioning is capable of voluntary control. What happens when an effort is made to channel, control, repress and/or depress a natural function by social control? The results of such control are not inevitable results, except for certain groups of individuals which at this time it is not possible to pre-identify. Thus, there is as yet no explanation for why, of four siblings in a family completely devoted to religious orthodoxy, sexual dysfunction was found in two as they matured, but not in the other two (or perhaps in one or three out of the four). As of now the sex therapist is in much the same situation as the general practitioner used to be when confronted by what was called a viral disease, meaning, "I don't know what it is, but it's infectious." Ultimately viral disease became reasonably well explained as better microscopic capabilities were developed. From a sociopathologic point of view, it is to be hoped that as capabilities become better developed in the study of human sexuality, an understanding of this innate "sensitivity" will emerge.

However, this much is clear: The difference seems to lie not solely in the religious environmental background (that, presumably, has been the same), but in the manner in which these "sensitive" people interpret the significance of what they hear—that is, in the way in which they have internalized their religious orientation, as contrasted to those generally who did not internalize this way. Why? Maybe sensitivity to the particular authority or to the way the authority presented the material.

Suffice it to say that those who internalize their religious orthodoxy in such a way that they interpret sex as sin, and/or sex as less than a natural function, and/or even more unfortunately, sex as dirty—these are the ones who later have difficulty with sexual responsiveness. Thus the problem is not simply with those individuals who approach marriage as virgins, but with those who approach marriage with virginity as a shield. For them, virginity has become not only something of innate import, but almost a way of life. Regardless of their particular specific theological orientation, these individuals are the ones who have the greatest difficulty in accepting help simply because they approach treatment with a totally false frame of reference. They represent, as a classification, the group with the poorest prognosis, for they are a group with no concept of sex as a natural function or of sexual functioning as a way and means of life. Sex for these individuals has become a performance, enjoined or permitted by a few words. That is tragic, because when sex becomes a performance, a thing to *do* rather than a way to *be,* it is no longer a natural function.

For example, for years psychotherapists, whatever their discipline, made the mistake of trying to teach or orient the dysfunctional male or female to accomplish something—the male to achieve and/or to maintain an erection to ejaculation, the female to become orgasmic. Yet these were all futile exercises from the perspective of the basic premise that there is no way to teach someone the respiratory function, that there is no way to teach bladder or bowel function, and, equally, that there is no way to teach sexual function.

Of course, in terms of effective therapy, one can remove the psychosocial roadblocks to effective function or at least aid in their abatement, but—accept it!—one can't teach the functioning itself. Any therapeutic attempt to teach this inevitably ends only in creating or reinforcing fear of failure and therefore abets inadequate performance. Here is where the individual's interpretation of religious orthodoxy can go awry. When one is imbued with the concept of a constant obligation to function professionally as the keeper of one's own morality, so to speak, and when this becomes a thing of such major import that the appropriate moment for its release is associated with a panic-stricken "What do I do now?" rather than with "Oh, boy!" the individual is in deep sexual trouble.

The Reproductive Biology Research Foundation is now seeing approximately one case a week of unconsummated marriage. These cases are coming literally from all over the world, and constitute some 20 to 25 per cent of the total case load. The shortest one has lasted about seven months, the longest over twenty years. This is an almost unbelievable length of time to be married without consummation. These are people with incredible levels of fear, with total lack of communication about sex. Sexual functioning in marriage can be, not constantly or even frequently but on occasion, the ultimate in communication between a man and a woman. That this level of sexual functioning is achieved so rarely is truly tragic. And one of the great reasons for this failure can be traced to the fact that the man and woman approach the authorized opportunity for sexual functioning after years and years of viewing sex as sin and as something we don't talk or communicate about. And, whether by hit or miss or by pure chance it doesn't work at first, they have no frame of reference within which to handle the tragedy into which they are locked.

In many of these cases of inability to establish interpersonal communication, to feel, to live, even to conceive of comfort and freedom in sexual exchange, the males have never learned to honor their sexuality; nor, obviously, have the females. When one can't honor one's sexuality, let alone one's sexual functioning, one cannot conceive of sex as a natural function, and one has no means of communicating other than through fear and frustration. These marital units are not married, so far as their ability to function is concerned, regardless of the words that have been said over them. Occasionally they do consummate their marriage, they may have a history of a dozen or two dozen consummations in ten or fifteen years. But to all intents and purposes they are still in the roommate category.

A Case Study

Many of the dynamics we have been discussing can be seen at work in the case we saw of an Orthodox rabbi and his wife with a marriage of some five or six years' duration, unconsummated because of his impotence. This man was the fourth son in a family of which the father and three older brothers were also Orthodox rabbis and the only daughter was married to a rabbi. No other career had, therefore, been possible to this man. His marriage opportunities were also restricted until he found a most attractive young woman whose father and only brother were Orthodox rabbis.

By the time we saw them, she had developed vaginismus.

However, under therapy the marriage was consummated not once but several times, the vaginismus disappeared and the man developed confidence. The feared difficulty would subsequently stem from the fact that with such a degree of orthodoxy, there would be a certain number of days every month when his wife would be unavailable to him. We knew that from a treatment point of view this could be tragic, for if a man has had successful intercourse only three or four times in his life he has overcome his extreme fears of performance to a degree but certainly not permanently. If he then has to wait almost two weeks until after the *mikvah* ceremony,* his inhibiting fears are almost sure to return. So we had to suggest to them that if they wished to continue effectively, they would for some time have to have sexual activity during the approximately half of each menstrual month that the *mikvah* would ordinarily prohibit. He was able to carry out this advice for about three months, except during her menstrual period, and even that five- or six-day delay occasioned difficulty for him. His guilt over the infraction of the abstinence rules was such that finally he reported to me that he would have to seek consultation. I suggested to him that he might present his case to a relatively impartial jurist. He chose the senior rabbi of the area, who ruled that the proscription against any manner of physical contact during the required period of abstinence must be maintained at all costs. It has now been around three years, and this man has never again been able to have an erection. So, although they consummated their marriage, this case must be counted as a statistical failure because they did not maintain effective function for five years.

We wish it might have been possible for us to have been involved in the consultation in some manner, and, indeed, we asked for this. But it was felt that ours was a prejudiced opinion, and we had to admit that it was. At all events, we were denied the opportunity; for this patricular religious community is reluctant to accept professional support or guidance.

With only two or three exceptions, courses taught in American medical schools about human sexual functioning date from

---

* Ritual bathing of the wife seven days after the end of her five-day menstrual period.

around 1960, and there yet remain approximately one third * of the medical schools in this country that give little or no recognition to this subject in their curricula. The situation is more dismal in the other professions. The subject of human sexuality simply has not been an acceptable or recognized subject for professional education, in spite of the fact that, as one of the natural functions, it should clearly be entitled to the same kind of scholarly approach and respect as have all others, not only in teaching but including definitive evaluation and a research orientation. Much is known about bladder function, for instance, and even more about bowel function, but almost nothing is known about sexual function. In the taking of medical histories each patient receives what is called a system review. This checks for symptoms in the respiratory, circulatory, digestive, urinary and reproductive systems. But in this system review *sexual* functioning is never mentioned, even though just five questions could cover it.

Sexual Questions for the Medical History †
1. Is the sexual part of your life living up to your expectations?
2. Is your sexual activity as frequent as you'd like?
   How often do you have sexual intercourse?
3. (For males) When did you begin to masturbate?
   (For females) When did you first stimulate yourself?
4. Have you had any sexual experience with members of your own sex?
5. Do you have any questions about sexual function?

If this is true in medicine, what about the other helping professions? It is the field of religious counseling that is called upon for help in the area of human sexual functioning and dysfunctioning more than any other discipline. The group that comes second in terms of demands is the large group of behavioral therapists—clinical psychologists and social workers, for instance. These, like the physicians, are now recognizing their own professional lack of training. Many individuals in these professions have, experientially of course, achieved a great deal of professional

---

* Since reduced to around 5 per cent.
† "Sexual Dysfunction and the Anxiety/Depression Syndrome." A round-table discussion with William H. Masters, M.D. and Virginia Johnson and members of their staff. Issued by Merck & Co. Inc., West Point, Pa., 1973.

know-how, but it's been by the sweat of their brows and on the basis of study and analysis of their own professional experience. As far as public needs are concerned, however, this is only a drop in the bucket.

So, as professionals, we must admit that till now we physicians have carried an incredibly false flag before the public about what we are supposed to know about sexual functioning. The one cheerful note in the whole situation is that profession after profession is recognizing this. In fact, that is what SIECUS is all about—to sensitize the various professions to their own needs and obligations for training in this area.

Still another point applying to our functioning as professionals relates to the inescapable fact that the male half of our population really don't know very much about the sexual functioning of the other, or female, half. It's terribly important that we, as professionals, acknowledge this, for if we males can bring ourselves to admit this without damaging our ego strength too much, then of course the same thing applies to women; for, despite their expertise role about themselves, they really don't know very much about male sexual functioning! If we can all bring ourselves to confront these inescapable facts, then we will have come far in presenting the concept of sex as a natural function to those who are in any way responsible for teaching at any level or for counseling, or for therapy.

The churches are in perhaps the key position to get the ball rolling. The concept of sex as a natural function is so new that no one has ever been aware of or lived with it as a concept. This means that in every religious orientation, regardless of its orthodoxy, sex has been so pulled out of context that the tremendous misconceptions that exist, the staggering amounts of misinformation that all of us accept as facts, can be reconstituted and reversed only by a tremendous effort. For example, every woman knows that the male is satisfied if he ejaculates. Every woman *knows* that. The mere fact that this isn't necessarily true never occurs to her, nor indeed may it occur to the male! Every man *knows* that as he ages, his sexual functioning will diminish, and we, as professionals, have done a great deal to perpetuate this myth among those who suffer most from it—the aging.

If the facts of sexual functioning were accepted, the attitudes and understanding of those professionals (especially the theologians) who deal with the subject might become so modified as to permit the concept that sexual functioning is an honorable role, to permeate the society. If that could happen, then whatever restrictions, from a social, moral, or ethical point of view were felt to be demanded, might be infinitely more constructively heard and internalized by those who are listening. For, as was pointed out earlier, it is exactly those who are listening, who have internalized what they have heard destructively rather than constructively within the framework of their particular personality make-ups, who have been made into sexual cripples. This is a responsibility that every one of us, as professionals, must accept.

Sex as Natural Function—and the Unethical Therapist

There is still one more aspect of this matter which must be mentioned. This is the responsibility of therapists never to take advantage of their professional background and the therapeutic situation to engender personal sexual opportunity from patients, clients or parishioners. This appears to us to be a major problem and in truth a despicable one. In perhaps one out of every six units consulting us there was a definitive history of sexual functioning on the part of one member of the unit with a prior therapist. We are indicting in this statement a roster of professions, including obstetricians, urologists, general practitioners, internists, a surgeon, pediatricians, psychologists, social workers, sociologists, priests, rabbis and ministers—each and every one of whom, male and female alike, when given the opportunity to function in the authoritative role of therapist, also took sexual advantage of this role in the guise of helping the patient with his or her sexual problem.

And the brutal fact is that even if this ploy was successful in the sense that the patient's particular sexual problem was resolved with that therapist, it did in no sense mean that this resolution could be transferred into effective sexual functioning with the patient's spouse—indeed, far from it!

It is vital that this information be laid on the line, because sexual interchange between therapists and patients appears to be at an unbelievable rate in this country. This statement applies across the board, because sexual interchange between male and female therapists with their male and female patients, and in both homosexual and heterosexual relationships, occurs constantly. Could some of the people reporting this be fantasying? Of course that is possible. But after hearing as many histories as we have, identifying and separating fact from fantasy in a high percentage of cases is easy. And even after subtracting the possible fantasy percentage, the figure remains at one out of every five or six cases. Why should this be?

In part the situation exists because these therapists, many with inadequate backgrounds, have been trying, perhaps with the best of intentions, to work with sexual dysfunction on the basis of their own *personal* experience. More importantly, these therapists still look upon the sexual function in terms of performance. And this betrayal of the professional relationship will probably continue until all professional levels accept, instead, that sex as a natural function is not one that can be taught.

Moral Reasoning and
Value Formation

Sexual Dilemmas at the High-School Level

CAROL GILLIGAN *

To speak about values and sex in a scientific context has generally meant to renounce, as Freud claims he did, any *weltanschauung* beyond the commitment to understand and explain the world as it is. Our pluralistic, democratic society encourages us to recognize different value systems—absolutistic, relativistic, hedonistic—as well as the range of attitudes these generate toward sexuality and its place in human life as "separate but equal."

The scientist's concern with causality has led us in this country to attempt to disentangle the causes of sexual pathology as we recognize it and to treat ignorance with knowledge and neurosis with therapy, all the while viewing changes in the culture with a hesitant mixture of hope and despair. In all of this, the ethical questions in human sexuality have been shunned. Focusing on the technology and pathology of sex, the scientist in his unease about questions of values has chosen silence.

To be concerned with moral development, however, means that it is necessary to see sexuality as an important area of moral choice in human life. Kohlberg has found that a sequence of stages characterizes the development of thinking about morality in general. Does this same sequence also characterize thinking about sexual relationships in particular?

* Carol Gilligan, Ph.D., Department of Psychology, Harvard University, Cambridge, Mass.

The Child as Agent

Piaget's conception of cognitive development provides the model from which our studies derive. In contrast with the social learning theorists who see the child as a passive receiver of messages from the environment, or the early Freudians who viewed the child as the victim of changing and conflicting instincts, Piaget observed him actively engaged in trying to make sense of the world. The continuing attempts by the child to apprehend reality form a recognizable and consistent sequence of cognitive stages, each of which has a logic and structure of its own and provides the child with a way of understanding the world. It is this logic that underlies the child's decision-making.

However, as children grow, both the world they live in and their capacity to deal with it become increasingly complex and differentiated. New experiences conflict with old ways of thinking which are inadequate to account for them and this disequilibrium spurs the developmental process by which the present and earlier stages are rejected and replaced by more adequate models. A list of those six stages with a description of each and the moral philosophy embodied in them will be found below. They should be clearly understood as being the basis for this presentation.

DEFINITION OF MORAL STAGES

I. PRECONVENTIONAL LEVEL

At this level the child is responsive to cultural rules and labels of good and bad, right or wrong, but interprets these labels in terms of either the physical or the hedonistic consequences of action (punishment, reward, exchange of favors) or in terms of the physical power of those who enunciate the rules and labels. The level is divided into the following two stages:

Stage 1: *The punishment and obedience orientation.* The physical consequences of action determine its goodness or badness regardless of the human meaning or value of these consequences. Avoidance of punishment and unquestioning deference to power are valued in their own right, not in terms of respect for an underlying moral order supported by punishment and authority (the latter being Stage 4).

Stage 2: *The instrumental relativist orientation.* Right action consists of that which instrumentally satisfies one's own needs and occasionally the needs of others. Human relations are viewed in terms like those of the market place. Elements of fairness, of reciprocity and equal sharing are present, but they are always interpreted in a physical, pragmatic way. Reciprocity is a matter of "you scratch my back and I'll scratch yours," not of loyalty, gratitude or justice.

II. CONVENTIONAL LEVEL

At this level, maintaining the expectations of the individual's family, group, or nation is perceived as valuable in its own right, regardless of immediate and obvious consequences. The attitude is not only one of conformity to personal expectations and social order, but of loyalty to it, of actively maintaining, supporting, and justifying the order and of identifying with the persons or group involved in it. At this level, there are the following two stages:

Stage 3: *The interpersonal concordance or "good boy—nice girl" orientation.* Good behavior is that which pleases or helps others and is approved by them. There is much conformity to stereotypical images of what is majority or "natural" behavior. Behavior is frequently judged by intention. "He means well" becomes important for the first time. One earns approval by being "nice."

Stage 4: *The "law and order" orientation.* There is orientation toward authority, fixed rules, and the maintenance of the social order. Right behavior consists of doing one's duty, showing respect for authority and maintaining the given social order for its own sake.

III. POST-CONVENTIONAL, AUTONOMOUS, OR PRINCIPLED LEVEL

At this level, there is a clear effort to define moral values and principles which have validity and application apart from the authority of the groups or persons holding these principles and apart from the individual's own identification with these groups. This level again has two stages:

Stage 5: *The social-contract legalistic orientation;* generally with utilitarian overtones. Right action tends to be defined in terms of general individual rights and in terms of standards which have been critically examined and agreed upon by the whole society. There is a clear awareness of the relativism of personal values and opinions and a corresponding emphasis upon procedural rules for reaching consensus. Aside from what is constitutionally and democratically agreed upon, the right is a matter of personal "values" and "opinion." The result is an emphasis upon the "legal point of view," but with an emphasis upon the possibility of changing law in terms of rational considerations of social utility, rather than freezing it in terms of Stage 4 "law and order". Outside the legal realm, free agreement, and contract is the binding element of obligation. This is the "official" morality of the American Government and Constitution.

Stage 6: *The universal ethical principle orientation.* Right is defined by the decision of conscience in accord with self-chosen ethical principles appealing to logical comprehensiveness, universality, and consistency. These principles are abstract and ethical, (the golden rule, the categorical imperative) they are not concrete moral rules like the Ten Commandments. At heart, these are universal principles of justice, of the reciprocity and equality of human rights and of respect for the dignity of human beings as individual persons.

To speak specifically of moral development is to refer to changes which occur in the process of thinking about right or wrong. The making of moral decisions is a universal feature of human social experience which can be structured in a finite number of ways, each representing a stage of moral judgment or a separate moral philosophy. Further, these stages occur in an invariant development sequence; each stage stems from the previous one and prepares the way for the subsequent one. Each successive stage thus represents a more differentiated and more adequate view of the social and moral world.

Empirically, these assumptions rest on fifteen years of research designed to show that cognitive and moral stages are real structures to be found in the development of thinking. The basic research strategy involves the presentation of hypothetical moral dilemmas and the analysis of the structure of reasoning used in resolving them.

In the United States, Great Britain, Taiwan, Yucatán, Turkey and Israel, it was found that the same basic moral concepts are used in making moral judgments, and the stages of their development are the same in every culture. Furthermore, experimental work has demonstrated that a child moves through these stages one by one and always in the same order. An individual may be found half in and half out of a particular stage, or may stop at any given stage and at any age, but if the individual continues to progress he or she *must* and *will* move in accord with the sequence of these stages. For instance, moral reasoning of the conventional type never occurs before an individual has passed through preconventional stage thought. No adult in Stage 4 has gone through Stage 6, but all Stage 6 adults have gone through Stage 4.

Sex and the Stages of Moral Reasoning

If moral stages define the structure of reasoning which underlies a person's thinking about such moral issues as the value of life, the value of love, of social welfare and responsibility, then the relevance to sex is apparent. Different stages of moral development describe different ways of thinking about sexual relationships and different philosophies as to the place of sex in human life.

In the description of stages there are three broad distinctions: the preconventional level of thinking, the conventional and the principled. At the preconventional level of moral reasoning, sex is considered from the point of view of the individual. He or she thinks about it in terms of its consequences, whether in terms of avoiding trouble or physical contamination or in terms of getting as much pleasure as possible. At the conventional (Stage 3 or 4) level of moral reasoning, sex is considered from the point of view of society, as something about which cultures have rules.

With the recognition of heterogeneity and hence of cultural relativism—that is, that more than one set of rules exists and each culture has its own—the conventional point of view breaks down and the individual is left with essentially one of two choices. He may decide that since all values are relative, there is no such thing as right or wrong and that it is everyone for himself, or he may come to understand that principles underlie rules and form the basis for a post-conventional morality.

Thus for the principled thinker, the rights and wrongs of sexual behavior derive from ethical principles concerning the relationship of human beings to one another in general. In other words, at the principled level of moral judgment, sex becomes "content"; no longer the subject of morality *per se* it becomes one of the many areas to which one can apply more general moral principles. When sexual ethics come to be seen as part of one's general principles for dealing with other people, then instead of asking if sex before marriage is right or wrong, one asks, "How can I relate to others in terms of their just rights and claims and in terms of their welfare?"

To ascertain the validity of applying moral stages to thinking about sexual relationships and their consequences, a study of moral reasoning about sexual dilemmas was conducted with a sample of 50 high-school juniors. Three dilemmas were presented: the first concerned the ethics of premarital sex, asking, "Is it right or wrong? why is it right or wrong? what makes it right or wrong?" and giving a series of contingencies which might affect this decision; the second dilemma examined the nature of sexual rights in marriage; and the third posed the problem of a high-school girl's pregnancy. With each of these dilemmas went a series of probing questions designed to elaborate the basis upon which rested the decisions of right and wrong.

In this study females interviewed female students and males interviewed males. We were able to differentiate in the responses to the sexual dilemmas the same stages of reasoning which characterize the responses to Kohlberg's standard moral dilemmas. Each stage reflects a particular moral logic which structures thinking about sexual behavior and its consequences.

In analyzing the responses, a basic differentiation was made between *content* and *structure* of thinking. Content consists of *specific attitudes,* such as, premarital sex is wrong or right. Structure is *the way of thinking* about these decisions of right and wrong. Premarital sex may be considered "wrong" because "you might get a bad disease from it," because it violates rules which are seen as legitimate.

In this particular sample of high-school juniors the level of reasoning on the sexual dilemmas ranged from Stage 2 through Stage 5. Taking responses to the premarital dilemma which concerns the rightness or wrongness of premarital intercourse, the following stage descriptions and examples indicate in part the nature of the differences between stages.

Sexual Reasoning in Six Stages

Stage 2 is oriented toward hedonistic satisfaction of one's wants and needs. Sex is like any other activity the self might either accept or reject. The attitude toward others is instrumental although limited by the recognition that it is wrong to hurt others in a concrete way or coerce them to act against their will.

Stage 2 has little or no notion of a relational responsibility generated by engaging in sexual acts, the individual does not invoke standards or generalized expectations shared with the partner, with the family, with the group or with the society.

Stage 2 reasoning is exemplified in the following response to the bare outlines of a story of a high-school boy and girl who found themselves alone and sexually tempted. What should they do and how should they go about making that decision? A typical Stage 2 response claimed that there is nothing wrong with pre-marital intercourse because "I think people can do whatever they want. The way they feel makes no difference, you can do what you want. It would be wrong if they had sexual intercourse without any thought of pregnancy because, just because of the inconveni-ence. A child could cause a lot of disturbance especially to kids of high-school age."

Stage 3, the first of the two levels of conventional moral judg-ment, is characterized by a concern with shared role expectations for sexual behavior—that is, toward being a good person of whom others would approve or a loving person for whom sex is an ex-pression of love. In Stage 3 thinking, conventional definitions of right and wrong serve to uphold group standards and maintain group approval. For example, at Stage 3, "It's O.K. as long as you do it as an act of love rather than as an act of sex." . . . "It goes back to whether there is any true love or not; if true love is involved I wouldn't say it's wrong. Sex is something beautiful, a form of communication." . . . "If a girl got pregnant her parents would be most upset and even her friends might shy away from her. It's still the moral behind it—I mean you can get away with it, but still you know you're not, like, clean any more." This is in contrast to the Stage 2 person who called a pregnancy bad be-cause it leads to inconvenience.

Stage 4, which with Stage 3 shares a conventional orientation, focuses on the issue of responsibility; to be a responsible member of society by following its rules, or to be responsible in one's sex-ual relationships in the sense of being in a position to accept the consequences of one's actions. In the high-school samples, Stage 4 judgments tended to see premarital sex as wrong either because it violated social or religious rules or because high-school students were considered too immature to assume responsibility for the possible consequences of sexual intercourse. Stage 4 may condone premarital sex where the individuals are old enough to assume this responsibility preferably within marriage. "If they were older and really knew what they were getting into, not just a passionate thing, then all right. If you are willing to accept the consequences—but in high school you're not really ready for it," or "I just can't believe in it, I think it's wrong because it's for after marriage and according to my religion I have to believe it."

Stage 5, the first of the post conventional orientations, differentiates morality from convention and orients toward mutual or contractual obligations, and derives responsibilities from agreements between the two people in deciding the rightness or wrongness of sex. Stage 5 accepts the relativism of specific institutions or beliefs, but recognizes the basic principle of mutual consent and trust as the decision-making prerogative. The relevance of law to sexual conduct lies in its function to protect the right of responsible rational consent, but law and authority should not legislate the particulars of sexual conduct between two consenting adults. This can be characterized as the civil rights attitude toward sex. The specifics of sexual relationships are seen as lying outside the moral domain. The moral principles of honesty and trust applicable to all human relationships guide judgment about sexual behavior.

A quotation illustrating Stage 5 thought: "As long as they are both honest and know each other's motives, I think that is the important thing, and what those motives are may make a difference in the meaning of the relationship, but as far as the moral issue of them being able to do it, I think it doesn't. I don't think anything between consenting partners is immoral whether they are homosexuals or—I don't know—dogs or people or anything. I myself don't generally get any pleasure out of sleeping with anyone I don't feel anything about, but I don't think it is immoral, it's just that I don't get any pleasure."

In this rapid review of the stages, the reference has been to the structure or process of reasoning about the morality of sexual relationships. The stages constitute distinctive modes of thinking about or solving the same problem at different levels of moral maturity. With the responses to the premarital story, an attempt was made to show how the same structure of thinking can produce differing choices as to the rightness or wrongness of premarital sex. Nevertheless individuals who reason at the conventional levels would be expected to hold more conventional attitudes toward sex than individuals at either the pre-conventional or the post-conventional levels.

The Moral Content of Sexual Attitudes

From the interviews, it was possible to construct an attitude scale and extract the content of attitudes—that is, *what* people thought was right or wrong. It was found as expected that Stage 3 and especially Stage 4 subjects held more conservative attitudes, with the girls being somewhat more conservative in general, as would be expected in this country.

The intention of this study initially was simply to show that it was possible to apply the same sequential moral stages to thinking about sexual relationships. However, there was one finding that is of particular interest. This concerns the issue of ethical relativism. It will be recalled that the rejection of conventional moral reasoning begins with the perception of cultural relativism, the awareness that any given society's or cultural group's definition of right and wrong, however legitimate, is only one among many— both in fact and in theory. To clarify the issue of moral relativism as perceived by an adolescent, students were asked the meaning of the term *immorality* and its relationship to sex. One answer: "Immoral is a strictly relative term which can be applied to almost any thought on a particular subject. If you have a man and a woman in bed, that's immoral, as opposed to the fact that if you were a Roman a few thousand years ago and you were used to orgies all the time, then it would not be immoral. Things vary, so that when you call something immoral it is relative to that society at that time and it varies frequently." The student would then be asked if he or she could think of any circumstances in which wrong in some abstract moral sense would be applicable. "Well, in that sense, the only thing that I could find wrong would be when you were hurting someone against their will," was a typical answer.

A further illustration of relativism: "I think one individual set of values is as good as the next individual set of values, you have a right to believe in what you believe in, but I don't think that you have a right to force it on other people."

The relativistic thinker is of particular interest, theoretically, because his crisis exemplifies the transition between conventional and principled thinking, and empirically because this type of thinking is so prevalent today. In 1969 Kohlberg and Kramer published a study entitled "Continuities and Discontinuities in

Childhood and Adult Moral Development." The most dramatic finding of that study was the apparent regression in level of moral thinking in 20 per cent of the subjects. These 20 per cent were among the most advanced in their level of moral reasoning at the end of high school, all having a mixture of conventional Stage 4 and principled Stage 5 moral thought. In their college sophomore year they rejected both their Stage 4 and Stage 5 morality and replaced it with what sounded like good old Stage 2 hedonistic relativism jazzed up with some philosophical and sociopolitical jargon, essentially saying that since all values are relative there is no such thing as morals and everyone can do what he wants. At the time of the Kohlberg and Kramer study, this drop in the level of moral thinking was labeled regression, fortunately corrected by time. By the age of 25, every single one of the regressors had returned to a Stage 5 morality with more Stage 5 social contract principle and less Stage 4 convention than in high school. All, too, were conventionally "moral" in behavior—at least as far as could be observed. In sum, this 20 per cent were among the highest in high school, the lowest in college and again among the highest at age 25. Moral relativism and nihilism seemed to be a transitional attitude in the movement from conventional to principled moral thinking.

In the present study of moral reasoning about sexual dilemmas in high school, related phenomena appeared. While the level of moral reasoning on sexual dilemmas was comparable to the level of reasoning on the standard Kohlberg dilemmas for about half the sample, it was lower for 80 per cent of the remainder. This means that these individuals showed what appeared to be a lower level of moral reasoning when asked to talk about the moral conflicts in sexual relationships than when talking about conflicts between life and property. In this discrepancy, the greatest decrement involved the usage of Stage 4 thinking. Individuals who resolved nonsexual dilemmas with Stage 4 reasoning were the ones who were most likely to use what appeared as a lower, predominantly Stage 2 hedonistic level of reasoning on the sexual dilemmas. Once again this suggests that the apparent regression to hedonism may be part of the transition from conventional to principled thinking. That this regression should first manifest itself in the sexual area may indicate the importance of this area in the confrontation between the adolescent and society. The sexual mores of the culture may be the first which are intensely experienced as restrictive, and thus it may be in this area that the individual begins to question the validity of conventional definitions of right and wrong.

Sexual Reasoning and Moral Growth

This questioning takes the form of relativism, but, when carefully examined, it is a different kind of relativism from that which underlies the naïve instrumental hedonism of the Stage 2 thinker. While the Stage 2 individual is aware that people judge and act differently, this for him is an empirical observation of how the world is. The relativism of the transitional individual reflects the knowledge of conventions which now come under critical scrutiny. It is a relativism which presupposes an internalized conscience, an internalized concern for rules which no longer are seen as adequate bases for moral judgment.

The question, then, is how developmentally to view this form of relativism. If it is transitional rather than regressive, we should not join those who deplore it and focus on its "amorality," but instead we should seize on its developmental potential.

However, not all questioning of convention is either principled or transitional. Only a minority of adolescents actually hold a post-conventional or principled view of morality and society, though many more live in a post-conventional culture. As an example, the majority of a sample of Haight-Ashbury hippies showed a mixture of preconventional Stage 2 and conventional Stage 3 thinking. While hippie culture appeared to be post-conventional, the thinking of its adherents was almost entirely a mixture of Stage 2 do-your-own-thing and Stage 3 be-nice-be-loving themes.

The hippie culture continually questions conventional morality, but on Stage 3 grounds of being harsh and mean, or on the Stage 2 grounds of "Why shouldn't I have fun," rather than in terms of the irrationality of convention itself. Thus many hippies belong to a counterculture which is largely conventional in its appeal, but which lacks the solidarity of traditionally conventional society. In other words, again we distinguish between *content* of cultural attitudes and the reasoning *process* on the basis of which they are either endorsed or rejected.

A Final Observation

A final observation is in order on the relation of moral thinking and reasoning to behavior. Previous attempts to predict moral behavior, whether on the basis of attitudes expressed or on the basis of "child-rearing" techniques, have been notoriously unsuccessful. Hartshorne and May (1928) concluded that honesty was not a character trait, but was situationally determined. In contrast, behavior in a college sit-in and in the Milgram (1963) experiment, as well as on standard cheating tests, has been predicted on the basis of maturity of moral judgment. Judgment-action relationships may thus be thought of not as the direct conformity of action to verbal moral attitudes, but as the correspondence between the general maturity of an individual's moral judgment and the maturity of his actions.

Moral judgment determines action by way of concrete definitions of rights and duties in a situation. Moral attitudes, as measured by attitude tests, do not indicate the way in which an individual defines moral conflict situations and in this sense their failure to affect actions is hardly surprising. Phrases like "Abortion is always wrong" or "It's good to be a virgin" if probed further turn out to mean, "Abortion is always wrong because you always get caught," (Stage 1), or "It's good to be a virgin because most nice girls are virgins," (Stage 3). Not surprisingly, then, a person who reasons at Stage 1 level has an abortion when there is no punishment or a Stage 3 girl has premarital intercourse when other "nice" girls are doing so.

Implicit in a Stage 3 definition of the good is the stereotypic conception of what most people do or expect, and this is more potent in defining the situational conditions of sexual behavior than are variations in the intensity of statements about the value of virginity. Sexual relationships and sexual behavior present moral dilemmas only insofar as they are seen to involve conflicting claims. How these claims are understood, how the conflict is formulated, how they are ordered—in other words, what the individual's priorities are and what choices ensue—are all influenced by the stable, cognitive dispositions which we call stages of moral judgment.

REFERENCES

Gilligan, C., Kohlberg, L., Lerner, J. and Belenky, M. "Moral Reasoning About Sexual Dilemmas: The Development of an Interview and Scoring System." Technical Report of the Commission on Obscenity and Pornography, Vol. 1, pp. 141–175.

Hartshorne, H. and May, M. A. "Studies in the Nature of Character." In Vol. 1: *Studies in Deceit.* Columbia University, Teachers College. New York: Macmillan, 1928.

Kohlberg, Lawrence. "Stage and Sequence: The Cognitive-Developmental Approach to Socialization." In Goslin, D., ed. *Handbook of Socialization Theory and Research.* Chicago: Rand McNally, 1969.

Kohlberg, L. and Kramer, R. "Continuities and Discontinuities in Childhood and Adult Moral Development." *Human Development,* 12, 1969, pp. 93–120.

Kohlberg, L. and Gilligan, C. "The Adolescent as Philosopher: The Discovery of the Self in a Post-conventional World." *Daedalus,* Fall 1971, pp. 1051–1087.

Milgram, S. "Behavioral Study of Obedience." *Journal of Abnormal and Social Psychology,* 1963, 67, pp. 371–378.

Moral Stages and Sex Education

LAWRENCE KOHLBERG *

A group at the Harvard School of Education is at work attempting to integrate psychological research, philosophic theory, and designs of educational curricula and methods into a viable approach to moral education. Parallel cooperative work in developmental moral education is being carried on in Canada by a group of philosophers, psychologists and educators (Beck, 1972). Experimental moral discussion programs conducted in the high schools as part of the ongoing project typically include discussions of sexual issues and dilemmas, since these are much on the minds of adolescents (Blatt, 1973). In work at the college level, discussion of moral sexual dilemmas has formed the heart of an experimental course in Family Life Education, being compared with courses which did not focus upon developmental moral discussion (Speicher, 1973).

Sexual dilemmas are approached as other moral dilemmas are approached—that is, in a developmental rather than a preaching or indoctrinative manner. Such an approach is distinctive in two ways. First, this developmental approach, while open and non-indoctrinative, is not relativistic, it does not rest on the assumption that "everyone has his own bag." Second, because it is based on a tested psychological theory rather than on a non-relativistic moral philosophy, its effectiveness can be measured. In fact, it has been shown to lead to marked and relatively long-range change in a

* Lawrence Kohlberg, Ph.D., Department of Psychology, Harvard University, Cambridge, Mass.

111

developmentally positive direction (Blatt, 1973; Speicher, 1973).

Particularly deserving of stress is the non-relativistic philosophic position about controversial moral issues in sex to which the project has led. The position is built on the fact that there exist culturally universal moral stages developing in an invariant order. The claim is made that the existence of these cultural universal stages helps to solve some problems about the relativity of values that have been worrying philosophers and educators for three thousand years. This relativity of values issue has been discussed in a general way elsewhere (Kohlberg, 1971, 1972), but it clearly has a specific reference to the problems of handling the value decisions in sex education and counseling.

The basic claim is that if there is a universal order of maturity in ways of thinking about moral dilemmas of sex, then it is legitimate for the educator or counselor to strive to stimulate the student to move to the next stage of development in thinking about these issues. This doesn't mean that the educator or counselor preaches his own values or the values of his church or group. It means that he engages a client or student in a process of thinking and dialogue about a moral issue of concern, and the process allows the client or student to move to the next stage of development in thinking about that issue.

Critique of Relativism

This raises the basic philosophical question of whether it is legitimate to stimulate change of moral thinking in the sexual area or any other in the direction of greater maturity, the problem of the relativity of values.

Certainly cultural relativism is one which does not stand up to philosophic or social scientific analysis, and it is that kind of relativism which is inconsistent with the finding of culturally universal moral stages. To clarify the issues, ask yourself to respond to one of the dilemmas used in our research.

In Europe a woman was near death from a special kind of cancer. There was one drug that the doctors thought might save her, a form of radium that a druggist in the same town had recently discovered. The drug was expensive to make, and the druggist was charging ten times what the drug cost him. He paid $200 for the radium and charged $2,000 for a small dose of the drug.

The sick woman's husband, Heinz, went to everyone he knew to borrow the money, but he could only get together about $1,000, or half the cost. He told the druggist that his wife was dying and asked him to sell it cheaper or let him pay later. But the druggist said, "No, I discovered the drug and I'm going to make money from it."

So the husband got desperate and broke into the man's store to steal the drug for his wife.

Now, Question No. 1 before the house is: "Should the husband have done it, was it right or wrong?" Question Number Two: "Do you believe that your choice that the act is right (or wrong) is a choice that is objectively and universally right, or is it just your personal moral opinion?"

Role of a Universal Moral Right

Two distinctions about relativism may be of some help here. First, if there is a universal moral right in this situation, it is relative to the situation. In general, it is wrong to steal, but in this situation the principles of human welfare and respect for persons seem to dictate a choice of stealing. Nevertheless, one can still say that these principles are universally morally valid, and that their application to this situation implies a decision to steal. There is a second distinction between relativism as a social science fact that different people do have different values and relativism as a philosophical claim that people ought to have different moral values, that no moral values are justified to all men.

The confusion of a typical sophisticated graduate student in one of the seminars is typical. She said in response to this dilemma, "I think he should steal the drug because if there is any such thing as a universal human value, it's the value of life and that would justify it." In other words, the student is saying what many would say, that the value of life is a higher value than the value of property and universally can be upheld. But when she was asked, "When you say 'universal value,' is there any such thing as a universal value?" she answered, "Well, all values are relative to your culture." And when she was pressed further as to whether the husband should steal the drug or not, she got all mixed up and said, "Well, it's up to him, if he likes her enough he should, if not he shouldn't."

The source of her confusion is apparent. She starts out by claiming that one ought to act in terms of universal value of human life, implying that human life is a universal value in the sense that it's logical and desirable for all men to respect all human life, that one can demonstrate to other men that it's logical and desirable to act in this way. Now, there is really no problem in logically demonstrating that value of life is a more basic value and should take priority over the value of property from any moral point of view. That issue of "ought" is quite distinct, however, from whether or not all human beings *do* treat life as of higher value than property.

It is not necessary to argue the exact philosophic basis for asserting that certain values or principles ought to be universal, but it is clear that cultural diversity is no argument against such universals. It is only an argument against moral universals if you think that your moral principles are equivalent to the rules of your culture or your traditions. This is what Sumner meant when he said, "Whatever the culture said was right, was right." For Sumner, slavery was morally right when it was practiced in Greece or in the United States because the majority of people thought it was right. Sumner, the leading ancestor of American anthropological relativists, used cultural relativism to support the notion that American capitalist imperialism at the turn of the century was right. If everything is relative, then all you've got is the rules of your culture maintaining your system as it is.

Significance of the Developmental Position

This extreme cultural relativist position is false. The work of the project demonstrates that in every culture the same basic values exist—values like Life, Law, Property, Contract, Trust, Affection, and so on. Furthermore, the major differences in ways of thinking about or upholding these values are defined by culturally universal stages which are found to occur in the same sequence in every culture. Now, these facts of cultural universality are not necessary to demonstrate philosophically the validity of ethical principles, but they are an extremely important basis for a philosophy of counseling and education which deals with values and bridges between the untenable positions of extreme absolutism and extreme relativism. An example of the problem is seen in the counseling approach which says to the counselee: "I'll be open, I'll tell you my moral position, then you go ahead and form your own decision." That certainly sounds good, open and honest but the counselor who adopts this stance must be asked a question: In presenting your own position, do you really think it's right or not and if you think it's right, do you think it would be right for the client to hold or not? If you don't think it's right for the client to hold, why do you think it's right for you to hold? And if you don't think it's right for the client to hold, how come you're expressing it? And if you do think it's right for the client to hold, why don't you say so instead of saying, "It's my opinion, but form your own decision."

It can be argued that you don't need moral stages to justify the notion that a moral decision like stealing the drug might be universally right. But even if that is the right decision in terms of a universal moral philosophy, it might not be legitimate to advocate this answer to students and counselees. Here is where the facts of universal development discovered by the project provide help. The developmental position says that while it is not justified to advocate strongly a specific decision or belief, it is justified to present a moral point of view and to attempt to get the client to understand the reasoning on which it is based. Such a presentation should occur in the context of a number of points of view and a clarification of the distinction between a decision and the reasons which underlie it. In practice, this is done in a classroom group in which the students themselves take a variety of points of view. Such a presentation of moral viewpoints aids in stimulating a more mature perspective rather than in direcly transmitting a "right answer." The approach is non-indoctrinative because it aims to stimulate the student to take the next step in his own development through a natural sequence. It rests on the natural tendency of the student to prefer the highest stage which he can comprehend— *a preference which has been shown to hold regardless of the prestige or authority of the teacher or counselor.*

The sense in which this developmental position helps solve the problem of relativism and indoctrination for the sex educator or counselor can be clarified by considering some alternative attempts to solve the problem. One attempted solution is to define moral values in terms of what has been called a bag of virtues—

an approach much used by educators in America in public schools, Sunday schools, and elsewhere. By a bag of virtues is meant a set of personality traits generally considered to be positive. Defining the aims of value education in terms of a set of virtues is as old as Aristotle and the attraction of the approach is evident. Although it is true that people can't agree on details of right or wrong, or perhaps even on fundamental moral principles, we all think we agree that such traits as honesty, openness and responsibility are good. We may not agree on whether premarital sex in high-school students is right or wrong but we can still agree that students ought to be responsible.

It is when the details of what makes up this bag of virtues are explored that trouble is encountered, however. In earlier days, chastity was one of the bag of virtues, but now it's not included any more. The bag of virtues has varied greatly through the ages. In traditional American character education, the basic traits were honesty, service and self-control. Aristotle's bag of virtues included temperance, liberality, pride, good temper, truthfulness and justice. The Boy Scout bag of virtues is well known—a Scout should be honest, loyal, and reverent and brave. One of the problems about the bag of virtues is that everybody has his own bag.

The problem runs deeper, however, than just what goes into the bag of virtues. It's what is meant by any one of them when its meaning is probed in any depth. Honesty and responsibility are good words and involve little controversy, but it's also true that a vague consensus on the goodness of these terms conceals very real disagreement about what they mean. What is one person's integrity is another person's stubbornness, what is one person's honesty and openness in expresing his true feelings is another person's insensitivity to the feelings of the other person.

The concept of responsibility provides an excellent example, since it is a sort of key word in many enlightened approaches in the value education field and it's a key word in many discussions. This concept says that sex education should encourage responsible decision-making, something that certainly all will agree to. But what does responsibility mean? For instance, most students engaging in student protest or civil disobedience consider that they have engaged in an act of social responsibility. However, the authorities at a university and the mass of Americans may consider that student protest constitutes a destruction of property and a violation of law and consider it clearly irresponsible.

Those who talk about responsible decision-making are not unaware of this problem. They define responsibility not in terms of what is done but in terms of the process of decision-making. In this sense, they are closer to an approach of this problem which orients to a mature or principled decision process. According to Christensen, (1969) a responsible decision is one ". . . made in the light of the evidence with an understanding of the consequences and with due consideration for others." The educator's role in aiding responsible decision-making is to stimulate consideration of the facts and of weighing the value consequences in the decision. In education, this is often called the "value clarification" approach. It is a useful approach as far as it goes, but it ends up in relativity. As stated by Dr. Christensen, the value clarification position holds that ". . . rather than imposing preconceived values upon a child, teachers need to teach the valuing process. This means listening to the student, giving him a clarifying instead of a preaching or commanding type of response, helping him to weigh alternatives and assisting him to identify and develop his own set of values in the light of this ongoing learning experience."

The importance of these processes is clear. But what it means to "develop his own set of values" and whether there is a standard for determining whether one set of values is more adequate than another must also be considered. The term "responsibility" does not help much as a standard to get us out of the relativistic morass. Simply to describe desirable decision processes as "responsible" leaves us lost in relativity. A decision could be made "responsibly" using any principle from the Stage 1 principle of "Don't get caught" to the Stage 6 principle of "Respect for persons and equity." In other words, the notion of responsible decision-making does not solve the question as to what is due consideration of others and what are the relevant consequences. That depends on the stage of moral judgment. As pointed out, acts of student protest, for example, could be "responsible" to the protester and "irresponsible" to the authorities. Nevertheless, if the individual student's decision process is examined, it can be determined whether the decision was made in "the light of the evidence and understanding of the consequences" and whether it involved "due consideration for others." Some students could probably be shown to have impulsively disregarded the facts and the welfare of others. However, for students who did make decisions "responsibly" and non-impulsively, there could be a wide variation in what would be considered the "relevant consequences" and what would be considered to represent "consideration for others."

Protection of civil liberties, for instance, was the consequence considered by the principled subjects in the Berkeley student sit-in. It turned out that the large majority (80 per cent) of the principled (Stage 6) students sat in, and in their interviews they indicated their concern about civil libertarian consequences. "Due consideration for others" for the principled students involved consideration of the civil liberties of others. In contrast to the principled students, only 15 per cent of the conventional stage students sat in. For Stage 4 law and order students, the consequences that counted were the disruption of order, the suspension of the activities of the university, and the delay in getting an education. "Understanding of the consequences" and "due consideration for others" were, for the Stage 5 and Stage 6 subjects, primarily a consideration of their liberties; but for the Stage 4 subjects the maintenance of the functioning of the system that they were in. Within their lights, however, students at each stage were responsible decision-makers with an understanding of consequences and due consideration for others.

The Place of Scientific Facts

With regard to "responsible decision-making," then, it is apparent that stimulating students to make decisions through considering the consequences in the light of the evidence and with due consideration of the welfare of others is a step, but it does not get far enough away from relativism in promoting a morally mature decision process. To promote mature decision processes, the attempt must be made to stimulate the development of underlying principles themselves.

This raises the more general issue of the role of a scientific understanding of the facts in sex education. An understanding of the facts is a basic component of sex education, and the kind of factual and cognitive enlightenment that SIECUS has promoted is extremely valuable. But it still must be pointed out that facts in themselves, and greater knowledge of the facts, will not resolve moral decisions in a satisfactory way without more adequate principles of moral judgment.

What do facts do? The chief contribution of science to moral questions is a) to clarify alternatives and b) to determine cause-effect relationships so that consequences of choice patterns will be evident. It must now be asked how and whether presenting scientific facts to students and clients will help them to make more adequate moral decisions.

It will be remembered that each of the moral stages or types considers a different set of facts central to moral decisions. When two people are at the same stage and disagree in moral choice, they will be able to come to agreement when both come to agree on the facts. As an example, Stage 5 utilitarians will agree that capital punishment should be abolished, if they agree that scientific studies show that it doesn't deter murder. Factual scientific clarification will not lead to agreement if there is a divergence of stage, however. Scientific studies of capital punishment are quite irrelevant to many Stage 4 subjects who believe that a murderer should suffer proportionately to what he did and never mind deterrence. The Harvard studies, while not irrelevant, are also not the major decision bases for Stage 6 persons who believe that capital punishment is a violation of the principle of respect for human life regardless of the statistics about deterrence.

What, in fact, can scientific factual studies of sex behavior contribute to an adolescent's moral decisions about sex?

What does the Harvard project propose? To encourage an analytic consideration of the factual consequences of decisions and the need for the individual student to generate his own position and his own reasons for it. This is done in the course of exposing kids to real and hypothetical dilemmas in which they discuss and argue with one another. And it has been found that this process of discussion and disagreement engenders uncertainty in the kids about their own thinking—what is called cognitive conflict. Once such conflict is engendered, exposure to thinking at the next stage above their own tends to lead to movement toward that next stage. In other words, in a discussion group which brings together, say, Stage 2, Stage 3 and Stage 4 kids, the Stage 3 kid will influence the thinking of the Stage 2 kid, but the reverse won't happen. Kids reject all levels of thinking below their own level even though they understand them because they have been through them. The same process can be observed in a variety of settings—college undergraduate classes, high-school classes, and even prisons. It is possible by this kind of discussion process to raise the level of the person's moral thinking.

A Concluding Case

This approach differs from the value clarification approach, then, not in giving right answers but in operating under the assumption that some answers, or rather some reasons, are more adequate than others. What this means in the area of sex needs clarification. Earlier, the dilemma of stealing the drug was used to illustrate the sense in which a decision could be right in some non-relative sense. It was right in the sense that adequate moral principles—principles of respect for persons, justice and human welfare—led in that particular situation to a particular choice. Some moral situations are not of that sort—moral principles apply to them but not in a universal way so as to lead to a definite choice. Sex behavior dilemmas, in particular, often lie in this region.

For example, a boy and girl fall in love in high school and get married right after graduation. They never had sexual relations before marriage. After they are married, the girl finds that she doesn't like sexual intercourse, so she decides not to have intercourse with her husband. Reluctantly her husband persuades her to go to a marriage counselor and she asks the marriage counselor, "Do I have an obligation to sleep with my husband? We want to stay married, but do I have an obligation to sleep with him?"

What should the counselor say? Does she have an obligation or not?

What about the husband? The wife says she wants to stay married and the husband says the same thing, but he goes on to say, "I met another girl and I want to have sexual relations with her. I asked my wife if she minded, since she wouldn't sleep with me, if I slept with somebody else and she said, 'No, it wouldn't bother her.' Is it all right for me to sleep with this other girl or would it be wrong?"

Would anybody take the view that there is a universal morally right answer to the question, "Does the wife have an obligation to sleep with her husband against her feelings?" or to the question, "Is it right or wrong to sleep with another woman if both she and the wife willingly consent to the arrangement?"

The answer would seem to be that while universal moral principles apply to the situation, they do not lead to a definite unambiguous decision or solution. The dilemma about sex is different from the dilemma about saving a life. The real problem is that nothing has been morally specified in the sexual situation. There really is nothing in the act of sex, *per se,* which is right or wrong. The information needed to determine rightness or wrongness of a choice from a moral point of view has not been supplied. The implications of this act are not clear in terms of respect for persons, equity or human welfare in these situations. As a result, clear obligations or rights or wrongs cannot be defined, although the situation is not morally neutral.

This example of how much tougher sexual dilemmas are in certain ways than the kinds of dilemmas frequently used to establish moral universals indicates one of the reasons why people who are concerned about sexual values tend to be more relativistic than people in other fields when they think about ethical issues.

REFERENCES

Beck, Clide. *Introduction to Ethics.* Toronto: McGraw-Hill Myerson, 1972.

Black, M. and Kohlberg, L. "Effects of Classroom Moral Discussion Upon Children's Leveling of Moral Judgment." *Merrill-Palmer Quarterly,* 1969.

Christensen, H. T. *Sex, Science and Values.* New York: SIECUS, 1969.

Kohlberg, L. and Turiel, E. "Psychological and Educational Practice." In *Moral Development and Moral Education.* Chicago: Scott-Foresman Co., 1974.

Kohlberg, L. and Turiel, E. "Psychological and Educational Practice." In Kohlberg, L., ed.: *Moralization: A Cognitive Developmental Process.* New York: Holt Co. in press for 1975.

Kohlberg, L. and Mayer, R. "Development and the Aim of Education." *J. Harvard Educational Review*, Vol. 42, No. 4, November 1972.

Speicher, M. E. "Stimulation Change and Moral Judgment: Experimental Validation on an Innovative Educational Approach to Sexual Morality." Unpublished Master's thesis. Purdue University, December 1973.

Evaluation and Prospect

Emerging Issues: A Dialogue

[On the final morning of the conference, only the representatives of the faith and denominational communities were present. Here follows a distillation of the major points made during the dialogue of that morning, the inconclusiveness of which led to an invitation to one of the participants, John L. Thomas, S.J., to prepare the final chapter. The note * below identifies those of the forty-five participants in this dialogue whose remarks are excerpted here. Ed.]

---

* Edward T. Auer, M.D., Professor of Psychiatry, chairman, Department of Neurology and Psychiatry, St. Louis University; Rev. Robert C. Baumiller, S.J., Ph.D., associate professor, Obstetrics and Gynecology, Georgetown University, Washington, D.C.; Rabbi Mordecai L. Brill, marriage and family counselor, American Foundation of Religion and Psychiatry, New York City; Mary S. Calderone, M.D., M.P.H., executive director, SIECUS, New York City; Rev. William H. Genné, M.A., B.D., coordinator of family ministries, National Council of Churches, New York City; Rev. Walter Imbiorski, The Cana Conference of Chicago, Chicago, Ill.; Rev. Boardman Kathan, Religion Education Assoc., New York City; Rev. William C. McFadden, S.J., S.T.D., chairman, Department of Theology, Georgetown University, Washington, D.C.; Rev. Harold W. Minor, Jr., Board of Christian Education, Presbyterian Church in the U.S., Richmond, Va.; Allen J. Moore, B.D., Ph.D., professor of religion and personality and education, Claremont School, Calif.; Aaron L. Rutledge, Th.D., director, Grosse Pointe Psychological Center, Mich.; Rabbi Jeshaia Schnitzer, Ed.D., Temple Shomrei Emunah, Montclair, N.J.; Rev. Robert H. Springer, S.J., S.T.D., associate professor, Christian Ethics, Woodstock College, N.Y.; William R. Stayton, Th.D., University of Pennsylvania Medical School, Department of Psychiatry, Division of Family Study, Philadelphia, Pa.; Dr. Harold Blake Walker, pastor emeritus, First Presbyterian Church, Evanston, Illinois.

MR. GENNÉ: What are some of the implications of this meeting? What are the steps that you wish had been added, or that you feel were overlooked?

DR. MOORE: First, the presupposition that religion is an enemy of sex needs to be questioned and re-examined. It is raised as often found among religionists as among researchers. My hunch is that if we had more data and could analyze them scientifically, we would find that the problem lies in how religion is internalized by cultural subgroups and that this is as significant a variable as religion *per se*.

Second, the need for religionists to facilitate some research in the sociology and psychology of religion, rather than leaving it entirely to social science.

Third, although everyone here comes out of theology in one way or another, I'm inclined to feel that we need greater research in our own disciplines and across religious lines. There is much confusion as to the history of the church regarding sexuality.

Fourth, we need a better understanding of sex as a natural function. This sounds great coming from Dr. Masters, but it has all kinds of theological ramifications, and poses all kinds of problems in theological communication.

DR. RUTLEDGE: There is the question of those influences on the growth and development of children that might later turn out to be detrimental to their mental, emotional or spiritual health. It is misleading to think only in terms of orthodoxy. Some of us remember going over this same ground when religion first discovered its interrelationship with mental health. But the church is only one force in our culture which tends to reinforce orthodoxy of whatever variety once it has been established. In the area of mental health legislation, particularly with regard to sex or many other controversial issues, the two groups which have been even more conservative than religion have been the law and medicine.

Tremendous forces operate within a culture so that once something is established as fact, procedure, theological idea or principle, or whatever, a composite of forces rallies to reinforce this and to insist that it never be changed. As one who has long been interested in both the psychology and the religion of life, I am most acutely concerned about what happens to turn any kind of instruction, guidance or teaching into a force that destroys humanity instead of creating healthy, spontaneous human beings. If we knew more about the differential responses to the same instruction as reflected in personality development, we would become healers, rather than tinkerers.

Another point: religionists and social-behavioral scientists have scarcely moved in their understanding of the formation, growth and function of conscience beyond the initial exploratory statements by Freud and the early philosophers. It will be in understanding how the superego grows and functions that we will discover how, reinforced by deprivation or trauma, people grow the kinds of consciences which turn the sexual arenas of their lives into a hell. They are their own accusers, arresting officers, judges, juries and executioners. Masters and Johnson were most explicit in saying that it is not so much the orthodoxy of the teaching as its interpretation by the individual.

RABBI SCHNITZER. As an individual standing outside Christianity, I too should like to comment on how religion is regarded as an "enemy" of sex. You realize what the division between the soul and the body has meant, and how the Interfaith Statement on Sex Education (see Appendix) does not have a chance to stand up against this tradition of two thousand years.

RABBI BRILL: I agree that the Interfaith Statement on Sex Education is only a kind of introductory effort that gave support to SIECUS and to others in the controversy over sex education. It is probably true that today there are many other areas that we share in a common cause. Perhaps we ought to think in terms of taking a next step, and to try to relate this idea of sex as a natural function to sex education so that it gets down to the level of parents and teachers. This is where we might hopefully reduce the distortion of growing lives. In other words, this should be seen as a form of preventive mental health in the field of sex so that, over the next generation, all of us, of whatever faith group, would see and teach sexuality as a natural, normal, healthy function.

DR. STAYTON: One of my expectations for this conference which did not come off was an effort to deal with the theology of sexuality under which we operate. Our present theology is neither relevant nor healthy, and yet it has been in use for several hundred years. We should take such new knowledge and assumptions as those from Masters and Johnson in terms of the naturalness of sexuality and from Gilligan and Kohlberg the material in terms of moral decision-making and with resources from the Roman Catholic, Protestant and Jewish groups we should develop a theology of sexuality which could then be used in terms of its implications for theological as well as for lay education. But we must begin by developing a theology of human sexuality.

DR. CALDERONE: As a scientist, I see this as the crux of the problem. Masters said something important for everyone to hear: whether in the name of religion or not, the expression of human sexuality has been interfered with. Remember that the Puritan ethic does not operate only among religious people. Quite the contrary. So, how are we to develop a theology that fits all the physiological and behavioral sexual data now available?

DR. STAYTON: It seems to me that the resources are right here and that we should begin the struggle.

DR. MOORE: As to "a theology of sexuality," my stance is that we must live for a long time with sexual pluralism, and that there presently exists no one theology, nor any one group that can form these presuppositions for a moral code for our society. In order for sexual pluralism to exist in a democratic society we have to surface the differences and identify the pluralism rather than attempt to cloak them in statements of goodwill such as the Interfaith Statement.

FATHER SPRINGER: On the possibility of some commonly acceptable theological statement, we would have to take into account the pluralism in theology not only among the various faith traditions but even within a given community. A basic theological statement would approach the whole question of human sexuality from a different viewpoint than an effort to deal simply with premarital and extramarital sex, for instance. One kind of approach would be sex and interpersonal relations. Another might be sex and the process of human growth and development.

DR. CALDERONE: I would like to see some of you grapple with this as one major block. The genital or erotic aspect of sex is, *per se,* a universal human drive as well as a major aspect of personality development, and is one of the most difficult areas in the whole gamut of sexuality. Whether among religious or among nonreligious people, it is difficult because it embraces eroticism from its beginnings in the newborn infant. This must be confronted some day and, hopefully, as soon as possible because it is where a prime difficulty lies.

MR. KATHAN: If Wardell Pomeroy were here he'd remind us that some of us in this room have given his books bad reviews, and still refuse to recommend them because of his stand on masturbation.

DR. CALDERONE: And on adolescent sexual experiencing as a part of development.

MR. KATHAN: Apropos of that, we might have more dialogue with the leaders of Eastern or other major religions which do not have the same problems regarding eroticism that we have in our Western culture. Recently at Harvard Divinity School a Third World Spiritual Summit Conference was held that included some of the outstanding leaders of Hinduism, Buddhism, Taoism and Sikhism as well as representatives of Islam, Judaism and Christianity. We need to remember that we are not only talking about the Protestant, Catholic and Jewish faiths—the three major religious groups of this country—but are also faced with the fact that other religions in this country are appealing to the younger generation.

FATHER McFADDEN: I see no difficulty in getting everybody to agree that from the point of view of religion, sex is a natural function and good. However, you will recall that Dr. Masters referred to a "misplacement" of the natural function of sex. This means he has an ethic of sexual behavior. It may be based on the findings of the physical sciences, and social sciences in combination with his own personal value-choices. In any case, he is able to come to the conclusion that some sexual acts are appropriately placed and others are misplaced.

This is where I see our differences coming to the fore. We can all agree on the natural goodness of sex, but what are the precise norms by which some sexual acts are approved and others are called misplaced? A particular religious tradition may, for all kinds of historical reasons, distort what is already present in its teachings about the goodness of sex.

No common statement can emerge until individual groups really get into that old question of what is meant by talking about the misplacement of a natural function.

FATHER BAUMILLER: You have just made an important point. Amid all of our breast beating, I think it should be pointed out that traditionally the church has been a defender of sexuality. Many of the things that have us tied up now had their origin in the defense of sexuality against some pretty weird and anti-sex kinds of heresies. There is a sense in which there is a clear recognition of the naturalness and goodness of sex in our beginnings, and our tie-ups have developed in part from our overreaction in the defense of sex. We very much need a better history of sexuality in the Christian tradition.

RABBI SCHNITZER: Father McFadden, do you think the Protestant, Catholic and Jewish disciplines could really make a theological statement undergirding and supporting that kind of thinking, without too much struggle?

FATHER MCFADDEN: If we never raised concrete issues such as homosexuality or premarital intercourse, yes. But once we get into these questions—well, it's not going to take place this morning.

DR. WALKER: I would like very much to see the church grapple with these problems on a theological level. I am aware of the difficulties that are involved. Nevertheless, I think that sooner or later we must lay a theological foundation for them.

FATHER BAUMILLER: Many things besides sexuality are natural functions, and in a way our job, our contribution to Masters and Johnson and others in sex research, is to tie together all equally natural functions into a coherent whole.

FATHER IMBIORSKI: The need for an accurate history about sexuality is important from another point of view. There are many things that we as religionists hold that we really need not, for they represent a cultural rather than a gospel heritage. In working with adults in my denomination, I find that simply setting forth where we have come from is a tremendous revelation. Very few of our people know any real religious history. Revealing to ourselves and to our people where we have been is tremendously useful.

Masters and Johnson made excellent points regarding the

goodness of sex as a natural function, but we should not become bedazzled by their focus, for sex has other uniquenesses that have yet to be considered. Aside from its procreative dimension, I'm suggesting that it is a very special kind of natural function or else we wouldn't be here worrying about it. In a sense, its potential for good or for evil is tremendous.

Kohlberg also did us a great service by at least beginning to give us some clues as to how we can get out of this absolutism-relativism dilemma. But we would be deluding ourselves if we thought he gave us answers. Instead he pointed to possible directions for continuing with the dialogue.

One other thing: we owe it to our traditions to investigate the ideals of commitment, of monogamy, of chastity, and to unpack the values in those traditions. If we can't say that a value in some way fits modern conceptual frameworks, then we should let go of it.

One of the most important things to do is to organize the questions, and some of this work has already been done—some of it in Europe, some in the Catholic tradition, much of it in the Protestant tradition. A coalition and organization of questions would be tremendously useful.

MR. MINOR: Whatever we do, I hope that we don't come out making sexuality so sacred and so holy that we separate it from human life and thus render it a disservice. We should not invest so much energy in theologizing that we don't get at the practical need for the development of sex education leaders in the life of our churches. As fallout from this conference, I would like to see educational work in sexuality, with theological seminaries and medical schools perhaps working jointly, that would be meaningful to students in both.

DR. CALDERONE: I cannot resist observing that throughout this discussion various ones of you keep failing to refer to the nursing and social work students, who are primarily female. You consistently speak in terms of male students, and I think this is a very serious and significant omission.

DR. AUER: We've heard how very little is known about sex by people who are leaders in the field of sexual research. Thus one of our greatest needs is an endorsement by theologians of the importance of further research. A number of us, however, have reservations about how much we ought to do about sex education at the present time. At this stage we are involved in a process, but are not yet ready to make dogmatic statements. At St. Louis University we are involved in introducing sex education to medical and divinity students, with techniques that we would not have used five or ten years ago because the faculties would not have allowed them. Such techniques involve the use of explicit films followed by open and direct conversations in group sessions. The results are interesting: one thing that surprised us was that these young students seem better able to deal with the explicit material than do many members of the faculty! We ask the medical students taking the course to bring their wives or girl friends if they wish, and they do. We try in this way to avoid the "smoker" effect of an all-male group and to have female points of view during the discussions.

FATHER BAUMILLER: I think it would be fair to say, first of all, that many of us are most enthusiastic about the Gilligan and Kohlberg presentations. This work presents a possible new framework in which our group can operate and a framework in which different faith groups can join in dialogue with a fresh start.

Secondly, the need for continuing education and development in the areas of moral thinking concerning sex has become, once again, very clear to us. Most of the people here are concerned with sex education within their church communities. There is a heartfelt need for a reassessment or a reworking of some areas that we learned as children to be unchangeable. We feel the need for guidance that will help us meet the challenge being presented by today's youth.

There is a feeling of change within our church on certain moral positions which used to be rather clear cut so that directives could be given with great assurance. But at present, young people are attuned to this change while their parents still insist on what they have been taught in the past even though it is actually no longer fully acceptable, either to many moral theologians or to the young people we are attempting to teach.

Something positive is emerging from these two days: a confidence gained when one realizes that, regardless of faith group, all of us see the same hesitancies, doubts and kinds of problems coming up from the churches and from older people.

The Road Ahead

JOHN L. THOMAS *

"Traveler, there is no path; paths are made by walking." *Antonio Machado*

Any conference designed to promote the interdisciplinary discussion of human sexuality and values is bound to conclude with more questions than answers. This can be all to the good and indeed may indicate considerable success, always provided, of course, that relevant concepts are clarified and the right questions are asked. As a long and varied historical experience attests, no two areas of major human concern have been more perennially perplexing than sexuality and values; and given our current sociocultural situation of extensive change and emerging pluralism, it seems safe to predict that this seemingly endemic perplexity will not be dissipated in the immediate future. Despite our best efforts, it may even be compounded for a time.

The purpose in calling attention to this somewhat disconcerting prospect is not to counsel despair but rather to suggest a *caveat*. The process of clarifying human sexual values evidently involves some uniquely problematic components. As indicated above, all known human societies have experienced difficulties in dealing with their sexual problems. None have been wholly successful in devising rational solutions, though their approaches have run the gamut from denigration and Stoic rejection to quasi-worship and Dionysian-like acceptance. Most have had to allow for a considerable degree of "patterned deviation" in the form

* Rev. John L. Thomas, S.J., Ph.D. Jesuit Center for Social Studies, Georgetown University, Washington, D.C.

of such openly tolerated discrepancies between ideal and practice as the double standard (there are no "fallen" men, only "fallen" women), prostitution, the keeping of mistresses, and relative promiscuity among various disenfranchised persons or classes. We have only very limited and empirically based information on the sexual mores of past generations, but the available evidence suggests that the gap between approved standards and actual practice was always considerable. Even the stern preaching of watchful Puritan divines, so it appears, proved ineffective in dissuading the elect from sinning sexually—it only kept them from enjoying it.

The Cultural Context

It would be quite presumptuous on our part to assume that we are far better prepared than any previous generation to deal with this process perceptively. As a matter of fact, there are several culturally specific grounds for concluding that in some respects we are less well prepared. To begin with, the profound malaise pervading the current climate of opinion regarding sexual values reflects a vague general awareness of a prolonged and still unresolved moral crisis. It would be superficial to view the present state of uncertainty and confusion as little more than perplexed concern with the personal maladjustments or transitory social imbalances resulting from lags or delays in adapting traditional ways of thinking and acting to the shifting requirements of our technologically advanced urban environment. Rather, it is becoming increasingly clear that we have gradually succeeded in rejecting past Victorian (Puritan and Jansenist—American style) sexual attitudes and norms only to discover that we lack a commonly acknowledged set of relevant beliefs and value premises on the basis of which we might formulate morally acceptable and compelling new goals and normative standards. Where there is no agreement on basic beliefs and value referents, there can be little agreement on a practical program of action. Particularly under conditions of democratic procedure, conflicting moral ideas and ideologies tend to neutralize each other in the public forum, since the concerted effort needed for shared thinking and acting is easily paralyzed by the diversity of opinions.

Furthermore, perhaps owing to the initial dominance of the Protestant Establishment, the spatial and social segregation of minorities, and uncritical faith in the acculturative efficacy of the "melting-pot" process, the American people have been remarkably slow in recognizing the profound implications of cultural pluralism. In particular, while acknowledging the ethnic, racial, social-class, regional and religious diversity within the nation, they have uniformly assumed that the vast majority of Americans share a common value system—in the sense that the values serving as their criteria for judging individual and societal actions, as well as for ranging a number of conflicting values in a hierarchy, are roughly similar. Although this convenient assumption is no longer tenable, given the widespread, organized and socially disruptive outbursts experienced during the past decade, many Americans are just beginning to discover that relatively large segments of the population have developed or are now developing life-styles and value priorities or hierarchies that reveal no common value system. Yet the Conference was not really prepared to come to grips with this issue.

Undoubtedly, this discovery that the melting-pot process has not fused us into a nation of like-minded equalitarians proves so upsetting because it undermines another widely held myth. When dealing with social disagreements and conflicts, Americans typically have assumed that all people are motivated primarily by material interests, and that these interests can be compromised or accommodated without jeopardizing essential values. In line with this pragmatic "business" mentality, it seemed logical to assume that rational behavior would imply that conflicts be resolved through open discussion of differences and mutual compromise of interests. Yet an analysis of the conflicts arising within a context of pluralism reveals that people may be motivated by values as well as by interests; and, further, that the contending parties may hold mutually incompatible value systems. In such situations, the resolution of conflict through mutual compromise would constitute a betrayal of underlying beliefs or principles, and not rational behavior. Conflicts originating in pluralism are basically conflicts of values; and conflicts of values necessarily lead to confrontation, as our recent painful experiences both at home and abroad clearly attest. In the practical order this means that when conflicts occur between individuals or groups, open discussion of the differences at issue can lead to workable compromises rather than polarizing confrontations only if the contending parties share a common underlying system of values and valuing.

These cultural blind spots; namely, our prolonged obtuseness to the far-reaching implications of pluralism as well as to the socially significant functions of values, have left us poorly prepared to deal with sexual diversity and change. As a matter of fact, we have responded to a rapidly changing social environment during the past half century by adopting new patterns of sexual conduct without duly considering whether the goals and purposes they necessarily imply are consonant with the broader framework of beliefs and values concerning love, marriage, the family, and life that we continue to profess. But adjustments made apart from a wider value frame of reference are aimless and meaningless. In the practical order, adjustments to change constitute a practical program of action—and programs of action, to the extent that they are rational, are conclusions based on the logical application of relevant principles or premises of values to sets of pertinent social facts. In other words, although our culture has predisposed us to become a nation of practical-minded problem-solvers open to novelty and change, it has not sensitized us to the continuing need for identifying clearly and making explicit the specific sexual goals and values we are seeking to implement. Considered against this broader cultural backdrop, the aims of this Conference appear so significant because they imply that we must give due consideration to all aspects of the human condition as we observe it in the existential order or, stated in different terms, that one does not change reality by arbitrarily ignoring or rejecting any of its constituent elements.

The Search for the "Fertile Zero"

Specifically, the Conference tried to face up to the challenge that the human phenomena included under the general rubrics of sexuality and values are complex multi-dimensional, dynamic components of the evolving human condition. As such, they not only affect, and are affected by, all the other basic components comprising this condition at a given period of history and within a given sociocultural context but they also lend themselves to analysis at many different levels and from many different conceptual perspectives. Moreover, whether we like it or not, men and women do constitute two possibilities of human nature, though their different qualities are neither clear-cut nor wholly symmetrical; and they do make decisions regarding practical programs of action on the basis of perceived facts and accepted values or conceptions of the desirable. The aims of the Conference imply that it would be irrational to deny, and irresponsible to ignore, any of these aspects of reality when we attempt to clarify our sexual values.

In the long run, it is more productive to meet, humbly and patiently, with other equally concerned (though diversely specialized) persons in a joint attempt to clarify the current dimensions of our knowledge and ignorance regarding sexuality and values so that we can then, hopefully, proceed to identify the real sources of our present predicament in their regard. Owing to existing differences in beliefs, values, and perspectives, of course such an approach may initially result in little more than a shared agreement to agree to disagree. Yet this in itself would be a positive gain, a kind of "fertile zero," in the sense that it provides the indispensable starting point for developing the mutual understanding, tolerance, and rationality needed to ensure effective dialogue on any morally sensitive, emotion-loaded issue under conditions of pluralism and change.

Inasmuch as the planners of this Conference obviously intended to move discussion beyond this "fertile zero" zone, it is only just to point out that they were attempting to advance through largely uncharted territory, without benefit of reliable guideposts or enlightening historical precedents.

Now, given the multi-disciplinary character of this Conference as well as the multi-faceted nature of its subject matter, it should be evident that the program designers faced some formidable problems. Should they include the perspectives of all the scholarly disciplines currently involved in the study of sexual behavior? And, if so, which school or schools of thought within each discipline? Should they place major emphasis on any one stage of the life-cycle? Should they proceed on the assumption that the traditional cultural prescriptions of heterosexuality, monogamy, and life-long conjugal commitment will remain dominant, or should they speculate about the possible form and functioning of human sexuality in a society in which these prescriptions are no longer of the first importance? Above all, should they provide for a formal presentation of the the different decision-matrices associated with the determination of sexual values in a pluralist society, or should they assume that these would emerge with sufficient clarity during the discussion of specific issues?

Owing to the innovative, exploratory character of the Conference, some of the preliminary judgments were based on more or less educated guesses, as is manifested not only by the issues that attracted major discussion but also by those that were overlooked or mentioned merely in passing. Hence, the following observations, based on a critical overview of the discussions, are made with an eye to future conferences and in the hope that they will serve a useful purpose by encouraging us to advance even further beyond the "fertile zero" zone from which we started.

In general, the Conference was never quite able to bring the discussions of sexuality and values into a clearly unified focus—that is, it was unable to get a good "fix" on some of those crucial points at which major contemporary sexual and ethical concerns presently intersect. In this respect, it is reminiscent of a number of similar conferences designed to discuss appropriate value-orientations in emerging new problem areas, such as genetics, medical research, managerial responsibility, atomic energy, etc. For the most part, the informative factual presentations revealed a limited awareness of the moral dimensions of the material, and consequently there was little concern to articulate its specifically ethical aspects; and the formal treatment of values tended either to be primarily descriptive or to focus on theory and processes apart from content.

In other words, although the Conference provided a good deal of useful information regarding significant aspects of sexuality and the developmental stages of moral reasoning, neither the authors of the formal papers nor the participants were prepared to orchestrate this material in such a way that pertinent value-questions would be brought sharply to the fore and the ethical implications of specific sexual issues delineated with sufficient clarity and detail to permit constructive discussion. This inability or failure is so characteristic of similar conferences that it suggests a cultural source. And, sure enough, this is found to be the case. For a number of historical reasons, modern scientists and philosophers have maintained such a sharp distinction between facts and values, between the *is* and the *ought,* that it has simply come to be taken for granted that science can furnish only knowledge of facts and factual relationships or means; while philosophy develops its own insights on values and ends or purposes without referring to the findings of science. As a result, in their formal presentations here, the scientists tended to show little awareness that one can ask value questions about their findings; and the philosopher discussants tended to confine their remarks to vague general principles, semantics, and more or less contentless moral processes.

Of course the real question in regard to the relationship between facts and values is not whether one can derive the *ought* from the *is*—that is, whether we can get ethical values from scientific facts. And until we are able to determine whether, how, and to what extent scientific knowledge may be applied in such a way as to clarify our values, future conference participants will continue to be exposed to interesting factual presentations and intriguing philosophical disquisitions without the likelihood of gaining much additional insight into the making of practical moral judgments in concrete historical situations. It is not necessary for our present purposes to spell out all the ways in which science enters into the making of moral judgments. Suffice it to say that every definition of morality, every moral system, and every conceptual model of the moral have built-in factual and philosophical (creedal) assumptions about the world and the nature of the human agent. Since the factual assumptions, at least, are based on the scientific knowledge (biological, psychological, social, and historical) available at the time, they are necessarily affected by the new insights that the steady development of scientific knowledge continuously provides.

This point is stressed because it throws a good deal of light on one of the major difficulties we face when making moral judgments in the area of human sexuality; namely, the initial structuring of the problem. In order to determine what is at issue, a mere description of the situation will not suffice; instead, we must analyze it in depth on the basis of the best scientific insights available.

Dr. Robert Jay Lifton of the Yale University Department of Psychiatry has stated the problem well. Since the behavior of individuals and human groups results from the three-way interplay of: a) the psychobiological potential common to all mankind at any particular period in time, b) those traits that are given special emphasis in a particular cultural tradition, and c) those traits that are related to contemporary historical forces, we must employ the best scientific knowledge available regarding these interacting factors if we are to structure a specific moral problem correctly.

In the present case, a careful rereading of the proceedings may very well lead to the conclusion that much of the difficulty associated with the determination of moral issues and the making of practical moral judgments experienced during the course of the Conference can be accounted for by deficiencies or inadequacies in the initial structuring of the problem. Briefly, there was need for a more comprehensive and explicitly formulated conception of human sexuality. And, second, there was insufficient understanding and appreciation of the way that contemporary historical forces are affecting the traditional sexual situation and all sex-associated institutions. As a result, the broader ethical and sociocultural contexts within which sexual problems currently develop (and therefore must be analyzed) were not articulated with the clarity and detail needed to identify the specific moral principles at issue or the feasible alternative choices presently available. Since these conclusions and the rationales underpinning them may not be wholly self-evident, it may prove helpful to develop them at greater length.

The Conception of Human Sexuality

Let us begin with the conception of human sexuality, mindful, of course, that the term *sex* is an abstraction, and that what we are dealing with in reality are sexed persons—that is, human individuals endowed with this distinctive attribute. Yet sex is a very fundamental dimension of human existence. Because of its connection with each individual's striving for personal fulfillment and the consequent need to establish satisfactory relationships with others, neither individuals nor societies can long avoid clarifying their stance in this regard. Individuals who attempt to give sex the "silent treatment" eventually discover that it has an uncomfortable way of reasserting itself, especially when it is most ignored. Societies which are unable to achieve general agreement on its nature and purposes soon find that their sexual mores are being determined by the unprincipled in art, literature, advertising and entertainment, who regard sex as a kind of enduring, providential seven-year-itch to be exploited for profit.

Granting that sex may have different meanings for different people and may even come to have different meanings for the same person at different stages of the life cycle, it is not this quality of relativity that renders human sexuality problematic. Past and present experience indicates that a major source of difficulty in understanding human sexuality is the tendency to take a partial or topical view of it, to see it in terms of only one of its dimensions, and to value only one of its many aspects. This seemingly endemic inability to view human sexuality as a connected whole perennially inhibits us from reacting to it with balanced, healthy openness. Following a segmented, topical approach, we attempt to deal with early sexuality, premarital and extramarital sexual experiences, marital relations, conjugal love, and parenthood as separate, unrelated items, and apart from the wider personal and social contexts within which they occur and in terms of which their real significance must be assessed.

An adequately comprehensive view of human sexuality implies, among other things, that we must keep in balanced focus the psycho-biological facts, their individual and social implications, and their interpreted meanings, i.e., the operative significance attributed to them in a given cultural frame of reference. Human sexuality is a complex phenomenon not only because it includes disjunctive though complementary individual attributes, and consequently couple-centered fulfillment, but also because one of the functions with which it is associated, the bearing and rearing of children, is closely related to group continuity and survival. The quality of being "sexed" has profound implications for both individuals and society. Sex never appears as a merely biological phenomenon or a psychologically compartmentalized series of acts. It is one element of the total personality, radically conditioned by this totality and the sociocultural environment within which the individual develops and seeks personal fulfillment.

Dimensions of Human Sexuality

Although we still lack fully satisfactory knowledge regarding most aspects of human sexuality, we can at least make sure that our approach includes all of its presently known dimensions. Considered from the viewpoint of the *species,* sex signifies that human nature, like all forms of mammalian life, is expressed disjunctively in male and female. In this sense, sex may be termed a generic disjunctive attribute of the species; "generic" signifies that it is an attribute shared by other species of mammals; while "disjunctive" indicates that the property of being sexed involves the possession of an incomplete though complementary generative system.

Considered from the viewpoint of the *individual,* sex appears both as a way of being and relating to the world and as a way of being and relating to others. As a way of being and relating to the world it is reflected at all levels of the person's activity: psycho-physical, psycho-social, and superpersonal or spiritual. As a way of being and relating to others it is reflected in the sexually specific, culturally defined statuses and roles in terms of which boys and girls in a given society are trained, and which later determine their relative social positions, accepted areas of action, and permitted aspirational goals or options as participating members of an adult community.

Considered from the viewpoint of *society,* sex appears as the basis of that primary human community of life and love variously designed to provide for the mutual development and happiness of the couple, the orderly fulfillment of their sexually associated needs, and the adequate recruitment of new members of society through responsible parenthood. Because the individual's reproductive incompleteness involves couple-centered fulfillment; and, above all, because the human infant is born utterly helpless, requiring a relatively long period of nurture, protection, training and affective development, some type of family system is found in all known societies. Such systems may differ widely, but they all include some recognized pattern of mating relationship, some form of ceremony or social arrangement assuring public acknowledgment of this relationship, some established procedure to provide needed economic support for the bearing and rearing of children, and some system of kinship designation defining how blood and marriage relatives are related to members of the nuclear family unit.

Considered in itself as a specifically reproductive attribute of the individual *person,* sex appears as a unified though complex system containing a number of components that for purposes of analysis may be studied separately. Among the more significant of these are what might be called its biological-constitutional components—that is, the hereditary, congenital and maturational factors reflected in its chromosomal, gonadal, hormonal, internal and external structural qualities, as well as in its characteristic pattern of growth-cycle, mechanisms of arousal, and erotic threshold. These elements are the essential "givens" of sex, setting limits to its adaptability and providing the basis for all subsequent psychosocial conditioning.

Our understanding of human sexuality must also take into consideration its sex-role components—that is, the behavioral patterns and psychological traits typical of each sex in a given sociocultural setting, and which the individual acquires or develops through social conditioning and learning experience. Closely associated with these are each person's genital-sex object preference, including the sources of genital-sex arousal, the goal and orientation of the genital-sex drive, and the nature of the object and situation within which genital gratification or orgasm occurs. Since the human genital-sex object preference is not innate but is learned, it admits of a relatively wide variety of expressions.

The Moral Dimensions of Human Sexuality

Indeed, we have now come to the point where we step into a quite new dimension, so far as human sexuality is concerned, for we now can see that it involves unique personal relationships. As we have indicated, the quality of being sexed in the individual person can be understood adequately only in relation to a reciprocal "other" sex, and it is ultimately on the basis of, or in terms of, this mutually complementary relationship that we tend to determine the meaning of sex. More important, mature sexual activity and fulfillment necessarily involves a relationship not merely to things but to persons. The mature, complete sexual act requires intimate union with a sexually complementary "other," and, as a potentially life-initiating process, may eventually involve still another in the person of a child. This inherent orientation to others endows sex with special moral significance, for these others are persons.

Thus, it may be possible, for an immediate and limited purpose, to distinguish between sexual behavior and sexual conduct. In this sense, behavior signifies objective, concrete activity; ranging, for example, from "wet dreams" to the act of intercourse, and thus including the relatively wide variety of actions that Kinsey characterized as "sexual outlets." Conduct, on the other hand, signifies activity as seen in its total human context—that is, it includes meanings and evaluations made in terms of values, purposes and normative standards. Therefore, it should be obvious that human sexuality cannot finally and adequately be comprehended simply as biological behavior. It always includes an inherent moral component, because the mature, complete sexual act, whether it is considered as couple-centered fulfillment or as a potentially life-initiating transaction, involves interaction between persons and unique interpersonal relationships. Any approach to human sexuality that does not take into consideration its culturally assigned meanings as well as moral dimensions must be regarded as radically incomplete and essentially inadequate.

Since human sexual goal-behavior is not innate or "built-in," we may expect to find that man's sexually associated relationships have been institutionalized in a wide variety of forms throughout the span of history.

On the other hand, history indicates that all known human societies have maintained some type of normative standards or code defining the appropriate expressions of sex for their members. In general, a review of the relevant cross-cultural data available indicates that past societies have followed two fairly well defined, though not mutually exclusive, approaches in formulating their systems of sexual control. The first may be called "society-centered," in the sense that it seeks to regulate only those expressions of sex that are considered potentially harmful to the welfare of the group. Because some control of sex is needed to maintain a society's reproductive, marriage, kinship, social status and ceremonial systems, regulations are formulated and maintained in terms of these systems.

Most historical cultures that developed outside the Jewish and Christian spheres of influence have followed this society-centered approach in developing their sexual codes. Inasmuch as the general welfare rather than sex itself is the major focus of concern, these codes are designed either to ensure social order or secure divine protection. Thus sex relations may be forbidden between certain classes or persons within the kinship group or immediate community, and before or during certain ritual celebrations, group activities or sacred seasons. Beyond these prohibitions, free sexual expression is permitted to the individual. In other words, sexual conduct becomes the object of moral concern only to the extent that it relates to group interests.

The second approach may be termed "person-centered" in the sense that it focuses concern on the individual and his personal responsibility for all voluntary, conscious use of his sexual faculties. Hence it seeks to develop normative standards covering all such expressions of sex under all circumstances. The use of sex in this personalist approach is evaluated primarily in terms of the perfection of the person; and, in practice, sexual controls will appear to focus on the sexual faculty itself rather than on those specific expressions of sex that the group may judge to be particularly disruptive of social order. This means that the deliberate, conscious use of sex will be regarded as morally good only to the extent that it conforms to what is believed to constitute the fulfillment of the person's divinely designed nature and destiny.

According to the first approach, only those uses of sex that have recognized social significance have moral relevance; according to the second, every willed, conscious use must be morally evaluated—that is, every thought, word and action concerned with sex is held to be regulated by a personally supervised code that is devised with respect to a creator, an integral destiny, and a social purpose. Both approaches lead to the development of a set of culturally standardized practices that range through definitely prescribed, preferred or permitted patterns of conduct to those that are definitely proscribed. With varying degrees of adequacy, both solve the perennial problem of reconciling the need for sexual control with the need for sexual expression; in each approach, however, solutions are developed on the basis of different conceptual starting points and premises of values.

Religion, Ethics and the Sexual Revolution

The two polar approaches must be kept in mind when studying the practical implications of the current "sex revolution." For the most part, the American people, as products of Western culture, have tended to follow and take for granted a person-centered approach in formulating their normative sexual standards. It is now becoming increasingly clear that large numbers are beginning to reject or seriously question these standards because they no longer accept the philosophical and theological assumptions upon which this personalist approach was initially founded. At the same time, since they appear either unwilling or incapable of undertaking the logical alternative of developing new sexual standards on the basis of a society-centered approach, the present sexual trend can perhaps best be characterized as a confused, uneasy drift toward normlessness.

At the very least, the situation demands that we think again about the relationship between religion and ethics. For it now appears that this relationship is not necessarily as direct as has sometimes been supposed. A glance at the history of the Christian churches proves enlightening in this regard. Their solutions to the moral issues generated by the Industrial Revolution, for example, provide little evidence of a direct, consistent relationship between ethics and religious doctrine; while a comparison of Latin American, Continental, and American Catholicism indicates that even Christian communities initially embracing similar religious beliefs may develop considerably different ethical viewpoints and patterns of moral conduct.

Indeed, we may take it as a general principle that the ethical perspectives and normative moral standards associated with a given religion will depend not only on the inherent logic of its doctrinal principles but also upon the sociocultural environment within which they are developed. The relationship between a religion and the ethical system associated with it and the society within which they live is a two-way street.

In an effort to explore the nature of this relationship more fully, we may define a system of ethics as a more or less integrated, hierarchically arranged set of general moral principles, together with the complex of related codes and norms representing the culturally defined application of these principles to the various categories of human action routinely encountered by the group. A developed ethical system defines both the morally acceptable ends of human activity and the means by which they are licitly to be achieved. In the final analysis, every ethical system implies a conception or image of man, the human agent. This image includes a set of beliefs regarding man's origin; his relationships to space and time; the essential qualities of his nature and, consequently of his orientation to his fellow men, society, and the world of nature; and, finally, his life purpose or destiny—that is, the desirable terminus of his development or fulfillment in the cosmic order as his group defines it. In other words, although all men recognize the quality of *oughtness* in human conduct, they define the specific contents of this oughtness on the basis of their distinctive image of the human person.

A religious system, on the other hand, may be defined as the complex of creed, cult, and code constituting a human group's total conception both of the group's relationships to the transcendent and of the practical consequences thought to stem from these relationships. Hence it includes a set of beliefs regarding a transcendent entity or entities having a significant relationship of supremacy over man and the human condition; a cluster of dogmas, myths and symbols embodying expressions of these beliefs; a cycle of sacred feasts, ceremonies and rites designed to assure doctrinal purity and continuity among the faithful; and a code of conduct covering activities prescribed or proscribed by creed and cult. In other words, it serves to determine the believer's position in the cosmic order by defining his relationships to time, nature, his fellow men and the divine, and thus answers his basic questions regarding who he is, whence he comes, and what he should strive to become.

Although the clarity and explicitness with which various religious systems answer these questions may differ in degree, they all provide their adherents with the essential components constituting their conception or image of the human person. Since this image is the ultimate starting point of all ethical systems, the relationship between religion and ethics becomes clear. To the extent that a given religion clarifies the basic components of the conception of man held by its adherents, it furnishes the indispensable ideological foundation for their system of ethics. This all adds up to saying that men develop their definitions of what is right or wrong in the practical order within a broader framework of value referents, organized into fairly consistent schemes or general patterns and related to their conception of man and the world. In addition to the formally prescribed and proscribed activities associated with creed and cult, a religious system affects the ethical judgments of the faithful primarily to the extent that it determines their conception of man.

But what is the nature of the ethical process by which these two systems are related in practical life? A general religious imperative such as the command to love one's neighbor as oneself acquires ethical significance in the practical order only when it is applied to specific human relationships in concrete situations. There are several possible way of making this application. For example, one may follow a system of casuistry and seek for precedents or directives in past religious documents regarded either as revealed or as the inspired *dicta* of great religious leaders; one may maintain that because the order of creation was vitiated by the Fall, it no longer reveals the divine plan, so that apart from the limited, explicit directives found in the Bible, the patterns of ethical ideals and normative standards we currently formulate must be regarded as relative, culture-bound products having no essential direct relationship to religious beliefs conceived as absolutes; or, finally, one may hold that the Creator's law can be discovered by human reason in the nature of things, and thus the ethical process is considered dynamic and existential in the sense that human reason, aided by insights drawn from revelation and tradition, strives to formulate appropriate patterns of ethical conduct in terms of the changing exigencies of the situation.

The far-reaching significance of different views regarding the ethical process appears most clearly today when the churches are confronted with wholly new situations. Although the major religious faiths in America have uniformly assumed that their beliefs had ethical relevance, it is becoming apparent that they are finding it increasingly difficult to demonstrate this relevance particularly in regard to sexual ethics. Because the social and cultural factors affecting sex, love, marriage and the family have been radically modified, the past provides few precedents for dealing with the present; while traditional conceptual frameworks are no longer adequate for developing authentic religious perspectives. This explains why I have judged it useful to outline this brief over-all view of the major dimensions of the problem, for these indicate not only the basic, elemental "givens" relating to human sexuality and its functions but also the diversity, variability, possibilities for rational intervention and consequent "degrees of freedom" associated with these givens as revealed in past sexual experience.

Although this summary description of my previously developed thinking in this area is admittedly sketchy and incomplete, it should suffice to indicate my reasons for concluding that discussions during the Conference would have been more fruitful if their initial starting point had been a more comprehensive conception of human sexuality—that is, one that included all of its relevant dimensions within its scope. To be sure, most of these facts and processes were either implied or explicitly noted at one point or another, but their full import was not always understood or fully appreciated because they had not been introduced systematically into the actual structuring of the problem at issue. Descriptive accounts of current scientific advances or of changing trends in sexual attitudes and practices may be highly interesting and instructive, yet by themselves they do not provide the extensive basis needed for the kind of consideration that must be brought to bear in the making of moral judgments.

Impact of Contemporary Historical Forces on the Sexual Situation

Let us turn now to the second, closely related conclusion that the far-reaching impact of contemporary historical forces affecting the traditional sexual situation and all sex-associated institutions was not given due consideration. For the most part, the discussion of sexual problems and values during the Conference remained largely within the traditional cultural frameworks relative to the structuring of cross-sex relationships, marriage, the family, and the over-all organization of the social system in general. Numerous and varied instances of change were implied or noted, of course, but, for the most part, these were regarded as quantitative rather than qualitative in nature. The discussions proceeded as if the current sexual situation was roughly similar to the perennial old situation though the incidence of some related problems had probably increased or, at least, had become better known statistically.

It is my firm conviction that a number of contemporary historical forces have already modified or are in the process of modifying key structural and ideological components of our traditional sex-related institutions to such an extent that the presently emerging sex situation is qualitatively different from the past and must consequently be analyzed within a different cultural frame of reference. Although it may be difficult to discern the future shape of things during this critical period of transition—indeed, it is not yet clear whether the rapidly shifting sexual attitudes and patterns we are witnessing signify a real sexual revolution or a mere passing revolt—I think that all perceptive observers will agree that social changes having strategic significance for the future form and functioning of human sexuality are already well under way, at least in all technologically advanced, highly industrialized Western societies.

It is necessary to mention only a few of these changes to make my point, but it may be helpful to add the reminder that sex does not exist in a vacuum, that human sexuality is always given meaning, and that conceptions of sexuality must be interpreted, functionally integrated, and structurally embodied in ongoing sociocultural systems. Thus, the drastic reduction in the family's procreative function, progressively rendered imperative by the recent continued rise in both the absolute increase of the world's population and the rate of increase, necessarily involves a number of basic structural and value changes that seriously challenge essential elements in traditional conceptions of sexuality and its family patternings and makes the future of these systems highly problematic.

What are the far-reaching individual and social implications of this limitation of reproduction considered as an essential component of the future human condition? Given the eventual imperative need for a generalized drastic curtailment of procreation, what types of personality structure, sexual relationships, and marriage and family forms will be functionally feasible? What types are most likely to emerge? Frankly, we have no way of knowing for sure. In the present state of the social sciences, we must rest content with more or less "educated guesses." Nevertheless, what we do know for certain is that we must now deal with a substantially new situation and that this entails, at a minimum, a comprehensive reappraisal and reformulation of long-standing conceptions of human sexuality, of the purposes and properties of marriage, and of the meaning of human sexual fulfillment.

In the practical order, this also entails a judicious redefinition and restructuring of sexual statuses and roles in marriage, society, and throughout the life cycle. In particular, owing to an impressive combination of changes—increased longevity, greatly reduced family size, earlier age at marriage, and the restriction of childbearing to the initial years of marriage—the relative portion of the average woman's total life-span devoted to bearing and rearing children has been greatly diminished. This situation gives rise to a number of presently unanswered questions. Are women to combine marriage with a job outside the home? Are young women to be trained for a career in the same manner as young men? Since advancement in one's career frequently involves an individual in spatial mobility, how feasible are two-career marriages? Modern couples enjoy a much longer marriage expectancy and a longer period of the "empty nest," how can they develop and maintain the kind of enduring companionship needed, particularly since their work experience usually involves them in separate "worlds" and the scope of their shared concern with children has been notably diminished? Now that the use of sex is largely separated from procreation and serves a primarily relational function, while its significance for women has shifted from the obligation of rendering the "debitum" to the right of equal enjoyment, what changes in values, attitudes, and normative standards are required to assure its function as a mutually supportive, unifying, unique expression of "coupleness" in marriage?

Finally, because successful participation in our complex, technologically advanced society requires a lengthy period of increasingly specialized formal preparation, modern young people must spend a good portion of their youthful years attending various types of educational institutions. This lengthened period of youthful dependency not only greatly increases the material and psychic costs of parenting, but places biologically mature young men and women in the difficult situation of having to cope with deep emotional involvements and sexual intimacy while spending long years of study and leisure together in a relatively closed academic subculture where they are excluded from responsible participation in the adult community.

These forces, and others that I have not mentioned, are now constituent elements of the present human condition and must be taken into consideration in any serious discussion of sexual values. Although the long-range implications of these historical forces are not yet evident, their present impact on our traditional sex situation and its related institutions is too apparent to be ignored.

Whether we like it or not, we must undertake the arduous task of clarifying our conceptions of human sexuality, of reappraising our cherished sexual values and their practical exigencies, and of devising feasible social structures for implementing these under conditions of rapid and extensive change as well as pluralism. This all adds up to saying that the aims and accomplishments of the present Conference are highly significant. The discussions definitely moved beyond the "fertile zero" zone of agreeing to disagree, and have opened the way to further progress in the future conferences which are so clearly and inevitably needed.

Appendix

Interfaith Statement on Sex Education*

Human sexuality is a gift of God, to be accepted with thanksgiving and used with reverence and joy. It is more than a mechanical instinct. Its many dimensions are intertwined with the total personality and character of the individual. Sex is a dynamic urge or power, arising from one's basic maleness or femaleness, and having complex physical, psychological and social dimensions. These dimensions, we affirm, must be shaped and guided by spiritual and moral considerations which derive from our Judeo-Christian heritage. The heritage teaches us that the source of values to guide human behavior is in God.

The sexual attitudes of children develop as part of their general social attitudes. Furthermore, respectful and considerate sexual attitudes help create healthy social attitudes. When the family and society view sex as loving and fulfilling, rather than prurient and exploitative, then both the social and sexual attitudes of children benefit. A healthful approach to sexual relations, willingness and ability to impart sexual information in a manner proportionate to the child's stage of development—these are among the elements which foster healthy sexual attitudes and behavior in the young. So, also, is resistance to social pressures which in some instances lead to premature sophistication or unhealthy attitudes in young people.

Responsibility for sex education belongs primarily to the child's parents or guardians. A home permeated by justice and love

---

* Approved June 8, 1968 by The National Council of Churches; The Synagogue Council of America; and The United States Catholic Conference.

153

is the seedbed of sound sexual development among all family members. Both the attitudes and the activities of the parents— toward each other and toward each child as an individual—affect this development. Healthy attitudes toward sex begin in the child's earliest years; they can best develop in an atmosphere that fosters in him a deep sense of his own self-worth, bolstered by love and understanding.

Sex education is not, however, only for the young; it is a life-long task whose aim is to help individuals develop their sexuality in a manner suited to their stage of life.

We recognize that some parents desire supplementary assistance from church or synagogue and from other agencies. Each community of faith should provide resources, leadership and opportunities as appropriate for its young people to learn about their development into manhood and womanhood, and for adults to grow in understanding of their roles as men and women in family and society in the light of their religious heritage.

In addition to parents and the religious community, the school and other community agencies can have a vital role in sex education in two particular ways:

1. They can integrate sound sexual information and attitudes with the total education which the child receives in social studies, civics, literature, history, home economics and the biological and behavioral sciences.

2. They can reach the large numbers of young people whose families have no religious identification but who need to understand their own sexuality and their role in society.

For those who would introduce sex education into the schools, however, the question of values and norms for sexual behavior is a problem—indeed, the most difficult problem. It is important that sex education not be reduced to the mere communication of information. Rather, this significant area of experience should be placed in a setting where rich human, personal and spiritual values can illuminate it and give it meaning. In such a setting, we are convinced it is not only possible but necessary to recognize certain basic moral principles, not as sectarian religious doctrine but as the moral heritage of Western civilization.

The challenge of resolving this problem of values in a pluralistic society makes it all the more imperative that communities planning to introduce sex education into the schools not only call upon educators to become involved in decisions about goals and techniques, but also invite parents and professionals in the community to take part in shaping such a curriculum.

To those groups responsible for developing school and community programs in sex education we suggest the following guidelines:

a) Such education should strive to create understanding and conviction that decisions about sexual behavior must be based on moral and ethical values, as well as on considerations of physical and emotional health, fear, pleasure, practical consequences, or concepts of personality development.

b) Such education must respect the cultural, familial and religious backgrounds and beliefs of individuals and must teach that the sexual development and behavior of each individual cannot take place in a vacuum but are instead related to the other aspects of his life and to his moral, ethical and religious codes.

c) It should point out how sex is distorted and exploited in our society and how this places heavy responsibility upon the individual, the family and institutions to cope in a constructive manner with the problem thus created.

d) It must recognize that in school sex education, insofar as it relates to moral and religious beliefs and values, complements the education conveyed through the family, the church or the synagogue. Sex education in the schools must proceed constructively, with understanding, tolerance and acceptance of difference.

e) It must stress the many points of harmony between moral values and beliefs about what is right and wrong that are held in common by the major religions on the one hand and generally accepted legal, social, psychological, medical and other values held in common by service professions and society generally.

f) Where strong differences of opinion exist on what is right and wrong sexual behavior, objective, informed and dignified discussion of both sides of such questions should be encouraged. However, in such cases, neither the sponsors of an educational program nor the teachers should attempt to give definite answers or to represent their personal moral and religious beliefs as the consensus of the major religions or of society generally.

g) Throughout such education human values and human dignity must be stressed as major bases for right and wrong; attitudes that build such respect should be encouraged as right, and those that tear down such respect should be condemned as wrong.

h) Such education should teach that sexuality is a part of the whole person and an aspect of his dignity as a human being.

i) It should teach that people who love each other try not to do anything that will harm each other.

j) It should teach that sexual intercourse within marriage offers the greatest possibility for personal fulfillment and social growth.

k) Finally, such a program of education must be based on sound content and must employ sound methods; it must be conducted by teachers and leaders qualified to do so by training and temperament.

The increased concern and interest in this vital area of human experience now manifested by parents, educators and religious leaders is cause for gratitude. We urge all to take a more active role—each in his own area of responsibility and competence—in promoting sound leadership and programs in sex education. We believe it possible to help our sons and daughters achieve a richer, fuller understanding of their sexuality, so that their children will enter a world where men and women live and work together in understanding, cooperation and love.

For Further Reading

Baily, D. S. *Sexual Relation in Christian Thought*. New York: Harper & Bros., 1959.

————. *Sexual Ethics*. New York: The Macmillan Company, 1963.

Calderone, Mary S. "Human Sexuality and the Quaker Conscience." Rufus Jones Lecture. Philadelphia: Friends General Conference, 1973.

Cole, W. G. *Sex and Love in the Bible*. New York: Association Press, 1959.

Duvall, S. M. *Men, Women, and Morals*. New York: Association Press, 1952.

Encyclopedia Judaica, *s.vv.* "Abortion," "Adoption," "Birth," "Circumcision," "Family," "Sex," "Women." Jerusalem: Keter Publishing Co., 1972.

Feldman, David M. *Birth Control in Jewish Law*. New York: New York University Press, 1968.

Feucht, Oscar E., ed. *Sex and the Church*. St. Louis, Mo.: Concordia Publishing House, 1961.

Greeley, Andrew M. *Sexual Intimacy*. Chicago: Thomas More Association, 1973.

Group of Friends. "Towards a Quaker View of Sex," rev. ed. London: Friends Home Service Committee, 1964.

Hathorn, R.; W. H. Genné, and M. Brill. *Marriage: An Interfaith Guide for All Couples*. New York: Association Press, 1970.

Hettlinger, Richard F. *Sex Isn't That Simple*. New York: Seabury Press, 1974

Holmes, Urban T. *The Sexual Person*. New York: Seabury Press, 1973.

Kennedy, Eugene C. *The New Sexuality*. New York: Doubleday & Co., Inc., 1972.

O'Neill, Robert P., and Michael P. Donovan. *Sexuality and Moral Responsibility*. Washington, D.C.: Corpus Instrimentorium, Inc., 1968.

Otto, Herbert A., ed. *Love Today*. New York: Association Press, 1972.

Patai, Rafael. *Sex and Family in the Bible and Middle East*. Garden City, N.Y.: Doubleday & Co., Inc., 1959.

Pittenger, W. Norman. *Making Sexuality Human*. Philadelphia: United Church Press, 1970.

Schauss, Hayyam. *The Lifetime of a Jew Throughout the Ages of Jewish History*. Cincinnati, Ohio: Union of American Hebrew Congregations, 1950.

Sex and Morality. A Report presented to the British Council of Churches. Philadelphia: Fortress Press, 1967.

"Sexuality and the Human Community." A Task Force study document published by the Office of the General Assembly of the United Presbyterian Church in the U.S.A., 475 Riverside Dr., New York, N.Y. 10027.

Siegel, Seymour. "Some Aspects of the Jewish Tradition's View of Sex" in *Jews and Divorce*, Jacob L. Freid, ed. New York: KTAV Publishing House, Inc., 1968.

United Presbyterian Church Advisory Council on Church and Society. "Dignity and Exploitation: Christian Reflections on Images of Sex in the 1970's." New York: Presbyterian Distribution Service, 1974

Wood, Frederic C. *Sex and the New Morality*. New York: Association Press, 1968.

Wynn, John C., ed. *Sex, Family and Society in Theological Focus*. New York: Association Press, 1966.

————. *Sexual Ethics and Christian Responsibility*. New York: Association Press, 1970.